Interest Groups
in American
National Politics

Interest Groups in American National Politics

An Overview

H. R. Mahood

The University of Memphis

Prentice Hall
Upper Saddle River, New Jersey 07458

Library of Congress Cataloging-in-Publication Data

MAHOOD, H. R.
  Interest groups in American national politics: an overview / H.R.
MAHOOD.
    p. cm.
  Includes bibliographical references.
  ISBN 0-13-914060-3 (pbk.)
    1. Lobbying—United States.   2. Pressure Groups—United States.
  I. Title.
  JK1118.M299   2000
  324'.4'0973—dc21   99-24488

Editorial director: *Charlyce Jones Owen*
Editor in chief: *Nancy Roberts*
Senior acquisitions editor: *Beth Gillett*
Editorial/production supervision: *Edie Riker*
Cover director: *Jayne Conte*
Cover design: *Bruce Kenselaar*
Buyer: *Benjamin D. Smith*
Editorial assistant: *Bryan Prybella*
Marketing manager: *Christopher DeJohn*

© 2000 by Prentice-Hall, Inc.
Upper Saddle River, New Jersey 07458

Printed in the United States of America

10   9   8   7   6   5   4   3   2

ISBN   0-13-914060-3

Prentice-Hall International (UK) Limited, *London*
Prentice-Hall of Australia Pty. Limited, *Sydney*
Prentice-Hall Canada Inc., *Toronto*
Prentice-Hall Hispanoamericana, S.A., *Mexico*
Prentice-Hall of India Private Limited, *New Delhi*
Prentice-Hall of Japan, Inc., *Tokyo*
Prentice-Hall Asia Pte.Ltd., *Singapore*
Editora Prentice-Hall do Brasil, Ltda., *Rio de Janeiro*

Contents

Part II: Lobbyists and Lobbying

Preface

Organized interests, or political interest groups, are permanent residents and actors in national policymaking. Virtually every segment of American society today has its spokesperson. Public officials at all levels—national, state, and local—are objects of a cacophony of interests lobbying for an endless variety of policy objectives. Certainly the years beyond 2000 will demonstrate similar patterns of government-interest-group interaction but the actors will vary over time.

This publication seeks to offer students of politics some insights into the formation, political strategies, and policy pursuits of the interest group universe. Fortunately, there is a growing body of interest group research that offers further insights to interest group behavior and what types of policies are being pursued. Just how various national policymakers respond to their petitioners is also being identified.

Chapter 1 concerns itself with both the structures and processes of our national political system as these have portent as to the relative success or failure of lobbying organizations. Chapter 2 looks at recently developed concepts about group formation, what sort of benefits they offer members and the role the national government has played in interest group formation. Chapter 3 offers a long listing and composition of many of the prominent organizations in today's politics.

Part II includes Chapters 4 and 5. Chapter 4 presents a detailed look at the process of lobbying and the lobbyists themselves. The latter are comprised of an elite group who play a vital role in representing various clients.

These individuals are quite knowledgeable in the "ways of Washington." They know who influences policy in government. Chapter 5 addresses the growing amounts of money that interest groups disperse in seeking political access to selected officials. Money does not necessarily "buy" influence but it does grant access that then offers opportunities for political influence.

Part III is comprised of the final four chapters of the book. Chapter 6 looks at the uniqueness of Congress and what strategies must be employed by organizations seeking to influence legislation. Congress offers various points of access such as committee hearings or mark-up sessions. Groups also spend resources on maintaining good working relationships with members of Congress as well as with their staffs. Chapter 7 addresses lobbying various executive personnel as well as the president. Given the growing of the executive branch with respect to policymaking and interpretation, interest groups are increasingly preoccupied with various agencies whose clientele they are. Chapter 8 examines the increasing importance of federal courts in policymaking. The growing agendas of both lower federal courts and the Supreme Court are the result of group lobbying. One must keep in mind, though, that judicial lobbying and legislative or executive lobbying call for different approaches by petitioners.

Chapter 9, the final chapter, attempts to predict interest group politics in the years beyond 2000. The chapter begins with a review of material from earlier chapters and uses this data as a basis for the predictions offered.

This publication does not try to judge "good" or "bad" interests nor does it offer a broad condemnation of the interest group universe. It must be kept in mind, all citizens under the Constitution, have the right to organize and petition. Certainly all citizens do not agree on what policy decisions must be made with respect to education, civil rights, or environmental issues. But, these and other citizen organizations do have the right to be heard and then government personnel must decide how to address or not address these concerns. The main purpose here is to enlighten readers of the existence of a virtually endless number of frequently clashing organizations. It is left to the individual to judge what role and contributions organized interests bring to American national politics.

I acknowledge with thanks the helpful comments of the following reviewers: Nancy H. Zingale, University of St. Thomas; Dr. Leonard G. Ritt, Northern Arizona University; and Scott R. Furlong, University of Wisconsin-Green Bay.

H. R. Mahood

Interest Groups
in American
National Politics

1

American Politics

Some Basic Aspects

INTRODUCTION

An enduring feature of our democratic society is the existence and inter-
play of many and various citizen interests. Freedom to organize and act on
behalf of aggregations of citizens goes hand in hand with an open, democratic system of government. This book is primarily concerned with formalized citizen aggregations or political interest groups. These numerous and
varied institutions are mainly interested in determining the content and
impact of various governmental policy decisions with respect to their memberships. (While there are thousands of organizations throughout the country, our primary concern is with those wanting access to or interaction with
government on a more or less continuing basis. Political parties are excluded
for the time being but will be discussed shortly.) Political interest groups
are found at all levels of government—national, state, and local. Political
processes and decisions have consequences for organized interests existing
at their respective levels.

　　With respect to what has been stated, an inevitable result of interest
group formation and activism is a preoccupation with government—legislative bodies, judicial forums, agencies, and so forth. These and other similar bodies have the power to tax, fund medical research, fight discrimination
in employment, or establish programs for the elderly. A high degree of government–interest group interaction is endemic to today's politics. Endless

numbers of public policymaking bodies function as fiduciary agents or legit-
imators of interest group claims.

But before we can begin to understand and appreciate the contributions and political role of organized interests in American politics, we need
to be aware of the unique characteristics of the American political system.
Its structures and processes have important political implications for the
relative effectiveness or ineffectiveness of organized interests as representatives of citizen aspirations. The balance of this chapter addresses a number
of attributes of American politics that have consequences for interest group
influence.

FEDERALISM

Decentralization of power, or federalism, is a basic characteristic of American
politics that modifies interest group behavior. Our Founding Fathers', fearful
of a potential demagogue or tyrant emerging, decentralized political power
in the 1787 Constitution. Political power is parceled out on three levels:
national, state, and local. Initially conceived as a way of preventing any
one level from dominating the other two, Washington has nonetheless
moved into a relatively more dominant position today.[1] However, public
officials at all three levels indulge in a good deal of policy or decision making such as levying and collecting taxes, building and maintaining roads
and highways, providing and maintaining healthcare delivery systems, and
operating various educational institutions.

Federalism, thus, allows different combinations of organized interests
to emerge and indulge in varying degrees of political activism. It actually
encourages interest group formation by providing many points of political
access (contacts with policymakers). State interests, for example, usually
concentrate their efforts on state administrators or legislators, while those at
the local level approach "city hall" with their concerns. All three levels have
their own interest constellations with their political agendas to pursue. Public officials at these various levels face a cacophony of organizations competing for influence.

THREE BRANCHES OF GOVERNMENT

A *constitutional division of power*—executive, legislative, judicial—is also an
important factor conditioning the amount of influence a single organization or coalition thereof may have. Borrowing from the French writer
Baron de Montesquieu, the Founders were determined that the system of
their creation would not allow the centralization of power that existed at
that period in France and England.[2] Their creation of a horizontal sharing

of power was unprecedented. Governing power could be controlled by dividing it among multiple branches and making the power of the branches interdependent.

These coequal branches maintain their own unique policymaking processes and procedures for dealing with various petitioners' claims. As later chapters show, Congress has such subsystems as committees and sub-committees; the executive branch has bureaus, agencies, and departments; the judiciary is comprised of different types and levels of judicial forums. As a result, this structural arrangement presents a series of difficult challenges to any interest group or organization advocating a significant policy change such as scrapping welfare assistance. In a case like this, advocates of change must operate across a broad governmental front that includes a host of officials scattered across branches of government as well as across various executing agencies. Power and policymaking capabilities are, thus, diffuse and require expenditures of a vast amount of time, effort, and other resources.

POLITICAL AND ECONOMIC CULTURE

Prevailing political and economic cultures also condition the degree of organizational success or failure, politically speaking. *Political culture* comprises a set of learned attitudes toward government and politics acquired over time. It involves an informal set of attitudes and values that determines acceptable or unacceptable political ideology and behavior. Characteristic of these are support for individual rights and equality of opportunity.

Most Americans have internalized basic constitutional rights of free speech, organization, and demonstration. Citizen organizations pursuing political goals operationalize these in their own unique ways. Groups utilizing the aforementioned rights are much more likely to achieve success over time than those that do not. A small minority resorting to violence or destruction of property risks alienating potential allies and/or public officials. Recalling the civil rights movement of the fifties and sixties, Martin Luther King's nonviolence concept found more public and governmental support than did Black Power advocates of violence and destruction.

Virtually all Americans agree that there should be equal opportunity for all in pursuit of their particular goals. Without this concept, various groups and individuals are perpetually doomed to failure and lack of political influence. Certainly, the concept of equality is not lost on women and racial minorities. As later pages demonstrate, coalitions of the foregoing are relatively better organized and politically more effective. Public acceptance of groups of citizens should not be stereotyped because of a common, unique characteristic. Commitment to equality for all, though elusive at times, is embedded in American culture.[3]

There are other attributes of political culture, but as implied here, they fulfill important needs for individuals, political institutions, and society in general. Political institutions (including political interest groups) gain an understanding of public expectations and see more clearly the contours of acceptable political behavior. The continuity of political culture brings greater predictability to politics and undergirds political stability.

Economic culture is another important determinant of interest group influence. In drafting the *Declaration of Independence,* Thomas Jefferson (borrowing from the British philosopher John Locke) proclaimed that people are endowed with certain "inalienable" rights—life, liberty, and the pursuit of happiness.[4] The latter phrase really implied property rights and literally became sacrosanct during America's colonial period. By the time of the Revolutionary War—with the abundance of free land, low taxes, and liberal inheritance laws—there was wide distribution of property among white males and a universal respect for property rights. In this context, the Revolutionary War can be seen as a property owners' revolt against the British crown whose taxes and trade policies were perceived as threatening colonial property rights.[5]

Deep respect for property rights undergirds the American capitalist system with its emphasis on private ownership of the means of production and on a free marketplace for the sale of goods and services. In this context, a strong Protestant ethic comes into play with its emphasis on hard work, thriftiness, individualism, and material success. This ethic influences public perception of the proper role of government in economic matters. For example, although we have been witnessing increasing public regulation of the nation's economy (such as manipulation of the nation's money supply by the Federal Reserve), there are limits. Only in times of serious economic duress—inflation, recession, or corporate monopolization—is increased regulation called for, and then, it is only temporary in nature.

Economic policy choices by Washington have important consequences for different interests. For example, a national agency may evoke certain licensing or regulatory powers to protect consumers from fraudulent advertising or dangerous products. Or Washington may use its powers to benefit certain private businesses by granting tax breaks or requiring that all car makers follow common standards when installing emission control devices. As long as fraud, unfair competition, or threats to worker safety are kept to a minimum, national power will not seek to intrude.

The nation's economy, however, is not static. In 200 years, its economy has evolved from an essentially rural, agricultural base to corporate urban manufacturing and then to postindustrialization. Industrial productivity in this last stage involves information and services. Fewer of today's workers are in factories or large plants; more and more are in education, health services, banking, and real estate. Facilitated by a modern information and communication system, America's work force is relatively more dispersed. This condition does not lend itself to the establishment and maintenance of traditional worker organizations. Rather, there is a tendency to establish ad hoc organizations to deal with problems such as job security, worker compensation, and workplace safety.

As this implies, a changing work force produces changes in its organizations. Whereas labor unions encompassed about 35 percent of the work force in the early 1950s, they encompass only about 11 percent now. (This is borne out by data in a later chapter.) Farmers, too, comprising about 2 percent of the population, lack the political influence they had in earlier decades. Though business has experienced criticism in recent years with respect to stock trading and corporate downsizing, its organizations continue to play important roles in national politics because of their relatively greater affluence, larger numbers, and increased competitiveness. Business organizations are heavily involved in electoral campaigns and have elected many of their supporters to policymaking systems (i.e., the Congress and various state and local positions).

Economic issues are of concern to all Americans and their respective membership organizations. The relatively more affluent not only perceive a greater stake in policy outcomes but have the resources to stay involved. Winning or losing in politics is often determined by the economic strength and aggressiveness that organizations bring to the struggle for influence.

Modern technology is also important because of its contributions to interest group maintenance as well as group formation. The eighties and nineties have witnessed a virtual explosion in the development and use of political technology. It is comprised of such elements as C-SPAN and CNN television, computer-based mailings, e-mail, Wide Area Telecommunications Service (WATS) lines, cellular telephones, videos, polling, fax machines, and the Internet. As a result, politically active individuals and organizations have an array of electronic means available for pursuing their agenda. Each organization, of course, chooses those most likely to enhance its political success.

New Right groups, for example, have been quick to exploit television. Paul Weyrich, leader of the National Committee for Survival of a Free Congress (NCSFC), has created National Empowerment Television (NET).[6] NET is a satellite network that allows members of the NCSFC to view public officials debating issues of concern and ask questions through an interactive connection. Weyrich believes that this type of instantaneous interaction has greater political advantages over letters and telegrams.

The Chamber of Commerce of the United States maintains a number of high-tech systems for both informing and activating its membership. The chamber publishes a weekly newsletter, *Washington Report,* that is sent to approximately 1 million readers and political allies; it also has a weekly television show, *It's Your Business,* that is carried on more than 100 stations and a radio show, *What's the Issue?*, that discusses issues of general concern to its membership. Finally, the chamber has Biznet, which is a closed-circuit, tax-exempt television network that can quickly activate the membership if need be.

The Internet, too, is extremely helpful in contacting legislative or executive personnel. Whether the computer user calls up an interest organization's Web or home page or receives political intelligence from automatic lists, it is quite easy to forward messages to targeted policymakers. These electronic mailings allow for instantaneous contact between private sector interests and certain Washington policymakers.

Modern technology also contributes to organizational establishment. It contributed, for example, to the establishment of Common Cause in the early 1970s.[7] The expansion of national television news in the 1960s made it possible for millions of Americans to view the vividness of the distant war in Vietnam with its tremendous physical destruction, loss of life, and the sad spectacle of hundreds of fleeing Vietnamese storming the American embassy in Saigon in their futile efforts to escape. The scenes and the war in general activated a constituency for a general purpose citizens' lobby made up of predominately middle-class professionals holding liberal social attitudes. Many of these individuals were looking for some way to express their growing dissatisfaction with the war but were not attracted to demonstrations or more radical protests.

Another contributing development was the relatively new process of computer-based direct mailing. In its early stages of development, Common Cause was able to mail millions of membership solicitations. Computers were also used to keep track of new members, break down the membership by congressional district, and facilitate local chapter organizing.

Finally, modern technology provided the organization with inexpensive, reliable, and quick long-distance telephoning. It was able to initially rent a dozen or so WATS lines that were used to communicate with members. These lines also periodically issued "alerts" that encouraged members to pressure congressional personnel on certain votes. New technologies, as we have just seen, trigger interest group formation. They also offer a new range of strategies that are available to today's interest groups while modifying older ones. In these and other ways, technology is changing the nature of politics as well as its outcomes.

The diminished role of political parties in American politics today offers opportunities for organized interests to play a greater role. Some 55 years ago, the late E. E. Schattschneider wrote:

> The rise of political parties is indubitably one of the principal distinguishing marks of modern government. The parties, in fact, have played a major role as makers of governments; more especially they have been makers of democratic government. It should be flatly stated at the outset that ... political parties created democracy and that modern democracy is unthinkable save in terms of the parties.[8]

A decade later, the American Political Science Association (1950) issued a report critical of state the of parties and called for a series of reforms to make them more "responsible."[9] The 1970s saw publications inferring that the "American party system was over."[10] More recent commentaries, though, have been more favorable to the continuing existence of the American two-party system.[11] Certainly, the persistence of the two-part system virtually over the entire history of the nation stands as testimony to its resiliency.

Political parties are best understood in terms of organizational theory.[12] Parties arose to meet certain needs of the new nation. Over time, as they achieved a life of their own, they often faced public criticism for not doing this or that as far as elections were concerned. But value-laden appraisals miss the point. Political parties are not good or evil per se; rather, they are functional. They are extraconstitutional institutions bridging the gap between public officials and voters.

Presently, there is an inverse relationship between political parties and interest groups. Weakening party loyalties and consistently low voter turnouts provide more opportunities for political influence by organized interests.[13] Initially, these two institutions complemented each other. Political parties nominated candidates, engaged in fund-raising, drafted and disseminated campaign literature, and indulged in get-out-the-vote drives on election day. (Earlier political machines were exemplars in this regard.) For their part, political interests endorsed candidates, disseminated party campaign materials to their memberships, and indulged in modest fund-raising activities.

Today, the situation is totally different. Organized interests are monopolizing the roles once played by parties with respect to identifying, endorsing, fund-raising, and campaigning on behalf of selected candidates. The upshot of this is that legislators, for example, are much more likely to ignore party leaders and positions and support interest group claims. This weakens the vitality of legislative parties. As a result, collective responsibility for decision making is diminished. Individual members are more susceptible to interest group claims, and the traditional processes of bargaining and compromise are virtually abandoned.

THE INTERRELATEDNESS OF POLITICS

American politics is best understood as an ongoing struggle for influence. In this process, what occurs in Congress can affect presidential decision making. Congressional consideration of an international treaty does not take place in a vacuum. White House personnel along with a range of other individuals and organizations are activated. The Panama Canal Treaty (1978) drew a wide range of individuals and organizations on both sides of the ratification issues. Concerned interests raised such issues as: Could the Panamanians operate the canal efficiently? What was the future status of American citizens living in the Canal Zone? What was to be done with revenues Panama would receive from canal operation? Since the United States built the Canal at the turn of the century, could it realistically withdraw from Panamanian politics?

To a degree, the interrelatedness of politics also determines organizational strategies. Individuals and organizations litigating before the Supreme Court employ one set of strategies while utilizing others when a presidential nominee is under consideration for appointment to the high court. A presidential appointment, incidentally, is made in the context of influencing future high court decisions through the appointment process. While Congress is considering environmental legislation, a certain coalition of groups will be active, but once the bill is finalized and signed by the president, that coalition will shift its emphases and strategies when approaching the Environmental Protection Agency, which both interprets and implements the new law.

The interrelatedness of politics also affects its makeup. The ratification struggle over the Equal Rights Amendment during the seventies and eighties activated thousands of women who were uninvolved on the sidelines. The greater enfranchisement of blacks as a result of the civil rights struggle of the fifties and sixties energized more of them to run for and be elected to office. This example is not lost on Hispanics and Asians who have recently come to America.

We explore many of these topics in the pages that follow.

NOTES

1. Paul Peterson, *The Price of Federalism* (Washington, DC: Brookings Institution, 1995).
2. Richard B. Morris, *The Forging of the Union 1781-1789* (New York: Harper and Row, 1987); Clinton Rossiter, *1787, The Great Convention* (New York: Macmillan, 1966).
3. See Jennifer Hochschild, "What's Fair: American Beliefs about Distributive Justice," (Cambridge, MA: Harvard University Press, 1981).
4. This phrase is found in John Locke's *Second Treatise on Civil Government* published in 1689.
5. Alan P. Grimes, "Conservative Revolution and Liberal Rhetoric: The Declaration of Independence," in *200 Years of the Republic in Retrospect,* William C. Harvard and Joseph L. Bernd, eds. (Charlottesville: University Press of Virginia, 1976), pp. 16–17.

6. Barbara Bardes, Mack C. Shelley III, and Steffen W. Schmidt, *American Government and Politics Today: The Essentials* (Belmont, CA: West/Wadsworth, 1998), p. 248.
7. Andrew S. McFarland, *Common Cause: Lobbying in the Public Interest* (Chatham, NJ: Chatham House, 1984), pp. 31–32.
8. E. E. Schattschneider, *Party Government* (New York: Holt, Rinehart and Winston, 1942), p. 1.
9. American Political Science Association, Committee on Political Parties, "Toward a More Responsible Two-Party System" (New York: Rinehart, 1950).
10. David Broder, *The Party's Over* (New York: Harper and Row, 1971).
11. Larry Sabato, *The Party's Just Beginning: Shaping Political Parties for America's Future* (Glenview, IL: Scott, Foresman, 1988).
12. L. Sandy Maisel, "Political Parties at the Century's End," in *The Parties Respond: Changes in American Parties and Campaigns,* L. Sandy Maisel, ed. (Boulder, CO: Westview Press, 1994), p. 380.
13. William J. Keefe, *Parties, Politics, and Public Policy in America,* 8th ed. (Washington, DC: CQ Press, 1995), p. 283.

2

Getting Organized

Some Concepts and Realities

INTRODUCTION

Current American politics are characterized by an endless number and variety formal and informal of interests. The constant clashing and competition among women, farmers, religious fundamentalists, homosexuals, smokers, and anti-abortionists ultimately produce some kind of policy response that bestows varying kinds of benefits among the competitors. Some will inevitably play a more significant role than others given the issues at hand and the resources expended. The political struggle is played on three levels—national, state, or local—and in various arenas or forums. It will not be totally or consistently dominated by one set of interests; rather, the kinds and numbers of interests involve conditions and determine policy outcomes.

Presently, our understanding and judgments of the roles and contributions of various competing interests are far from complete. There is no comprehensive body of literature or data called "group theory." James Madison, our fourth president, is widely considered one of the nation's foremost political theorists. His views are expounded brilliantly in *The Federalist,* a series of papers by Alexander Hamilton, James Madison, and John Jay written in connection with the ratification struggle of the 1787 Constitution. Perhaps the most famous of *The Federalist* papers is No. 10, written by Madison. He was concerned, after the political conflicts under the older Articles of Confederation made government unworkable, primarily with government stability and the problems posed by what he termed "the violence and mischiefs of faction." Factions are dangerous, Madison believed, because they inflame passions, encourage selfish interests, and excite mutual animosities that threaten the "common good." But to remove the causes of factions "by destroying the liberty which is essential to its existence is worse than the disease." This is the Madisonian dilemma. Madison concluded that one cannot control the causes of factions, but one can design a government that can control their effects. Madison is, therefore, the first to publicly perceive incipient factions emerging in the new nation. Rather than trying to inhibit factions, his plan (incorporated in the new Constitution) called for a system of checks and balances that would countervail the political capabilities of the emerging factions. Madison's prescriptions, though, represent only a small step toward some kind of interest group theory.

THE ADVENT OF INTEREST GROUP THEORY: ARTHUR BENTLEY AND DAVID TRUMAN

The earliest discourse on political interest groups in the twentieth century was by Arthur Bentley in his *The Process of Government* (1908).[1] A sociologist by training, Bentley offers a rudimentary introduction to the study of political interest groups. Arguing that existing studies of politics and government were both static and unrealistic, Bentley called for a new and radical approach. The "stuff of politics and government were not structures and laws but interest groups and their activity." Society is nothing other than the complex arrangement of groups that compose it. Table 2.1 offers a brief analysis of early pluralist commentators.

For Bentley, interest groups were not merely sociological entities capable of influencing government occasionally. Indeed, their influence was pervasive. American politics were group politics, and vice versa:

> We shall have to take all these political groups, and get them started with their meaning, with their value, with their representative quality. We shall have to get hold of political institutions, legislatures, courts, executive officers, and get them started as groups, and in terms of groups.[2]

Thus, Bentley argued that within Madison's concept of factions lay the seeds for a theory of modern democratic government whose driving force was competition among numerous groups. Bentley stressed the representative virtues inherent in the struggle among a "plurality" of interest groups. He believed individual autonomy was nonexistent as a source of political awareness. One's political preferences grew out of group affiliations and

TABLE 2.1 Pluralist Critiques

Theory	Theorist	Assumption	Critique
Conflict Theory	Arthur Bentley (*The Process of Government*, 1908)	Public policies emanate from competing interest groups.	Government referees and ratifies interest group victories and losses.
Group Formation	Pendleton Herring (*Group Representation Before Congress*, 1929)	Interest group formation occurs in waves.	Emergence of groups and their activities are mainly defensive in nature.
Disturbance Theory	David Truman (*Governmental Process*, 1951)	Socioeconomic disturbances lead to group formation.	Socioeconomic changes modify the existing status quo among groups.
Exchange Theory	Robert Salisbury, ed. (*Interest Group Politics in America*, 1970)	Group formation is based on an exchange of benefits between an entrepreneur/organizer and the rank and file.	For group viability, it is necessary to maintain an adequate flow of tangible and intangible benefits to both the members and organizers.

identifications and the demands and expectations engendered by those associations.

Government processes and outcomes, along with political parties and public opinion, are all outgrowths of governmental forces at work. All three branches of government operate primarily as mediators between government and competing private interests that are pressing upon government. Governmental units are means of adjusting and reconciling the various group demands.

It was Bentley, then, who first foresaw the pluralist world of constant and ongoing competition among groups. These, incidentally, were forming, re-forming, merging, splitting, and so on, but in the end somehow attaining some kind of policy response. In this array of groups, Bentley also saw the importance of political parties. They played a representative function as "organizations of voters brought together to act as a representative of the underlying interest groups in which these voters ... present themselves."[3] They serve as means for interests to gain political leverage through the electoral process.

Bentley's political discourse of interest groups went largely unheeded by his peers. Though it was polemical, *The Process of Government* represented a challenge to social scientists of that day, but discourses on politics continued in the same manner.

A more recent pluralist advocate is David Truman. Truman is responsible for resurrecting Bentley's thesis of politics in his work *The Governmental Process* (1951).[4] He offers a relatively more empirically based rationale than Bentley. American politics and government involve a complex set of interactions and bargaining among a panoply of diverse interests. "The group experiences and affiliations of the individual are the primary ... means by which the individual knows, interprets, and reacts to the society in which he exists."[5]

Although Truman's emphasis is on organized interest groups, he acknowledges the existence of latent interests and groups that emerge in the face of some outside threat. A strong point of Truman's analysis is his survey of the history of group formation. When the existence of the political status quo is threatened—wars, immigration, changes in economic forces—new groups emerge. These transformations of the group universe occur in waves, such as what occurred in the civil rights and environmental movements of the 1960s. The number and existence of groups in a society, according to Truman, "serve as an index of stability" within a society, and their number may be used as an index of its complexity.

Truman had a somewhat idealized version of the democratic nature of political interest groups. He assumed, for purposes of effective political action, that all groups would adopt and maintain a democratic mold. This, in turn, would produce various alliances and coalitions of interests that represented the public good. This democratic underpinning is central to Truman's concept of politics.

In this context, then, the prime objective of political organizations is to influence public policymaking. Policy outcomes are the results of interest groups bringing pressures to bear at various key points of the political process. Alliance building, horse trading, and logrolling in the legislative process, for example, are indicative of group access. Vote trading and the give-and-take between constituent claims and White House pressures are the traditional ways of resolving group claims. Seen in this light, these interactions are deemed legitimate ways of adjusting conflicting interests in society.

The publication of *The Governmental Process* sparked a renaissance of Bentley's thesis and produced a new generation of political scientists investigating the formation and political activism of political interest groups—Jeffrey Berry, William Browne, Allen Cigler, Robert Dahl, Earl Latham, Burdette Loomis, Andrew McFarland, Terry Moe, Robert Salisbury, Kay Schlozman, John Tierney, Clement Vose, and Harmon Zeigler—to name a few. In a general sense, these writers perceive American politics in pluralistic terms (i.e., that politics is very much influenced by the existence and political activism of many political interest groups and that by studying group activity one is studying the "real world" of politics and policymaking).

A number of tenets emerging from this new emphasis on political interest groups undergird the concept of political pluralism. First, our political system is essentially group-based. The distribution of power and policy formation stem from the existing equilibrium of competing groups. Second, the demands of a pluralistic society are achieved through group interaction and competition. A consensus is attained through a complex process of competing interest groups, issues, points of access, and resource availability. These converge and produce the common good. The state of equilibrium changes when new groups emerge and assert themselves for purposes of gaining some benefit. Third, the political arena is dynamic. Decisions arrived at (e.g., court decisions or the passage of laws) may be modified by subsequent group actions not in agreement with previous decisions. Further points of political access or contact are essentially open. As Robert Dahl has written, "the independence, penetrability, and heterogeneity of the various segments of the political stratum all but guarantee that any dissatisfied group will find spokesmen in the political stratum."[6] Finally, pluralism assumes a system of widely dispersed resources with power and influence distributed broadly across a range of groups. No one set of interests is capable of totally dominating the decision making process.

CRITICS AND CRITICISMS OF PLURALISM AND INTEREST GROUP THEORIES

It was inevitable, of course, that these concepts would engender a host of critics. Antipluralists raise a number of questions with respect to the reliability of pluralist claims such as: How do interest groups become established? How well do interest group represent their memberships? Is there really political parity among interest groups as far as influence is concerned? Are public policymaking centers easily penetrated by all organized interests? Like their counterparts, antipluralists also operate from different theoretical bases in their evaluations of groups in the political process.

A brief commentary on a few of these critics is in order. Antipluralist critics fall into two camps: those who have normative or theoretical objections and those who have methodological or empirical objections. Characteristic of the first are Ted Lowi and the late E. E. Schattschneider. Lowi coined the phrase "interest group liberalism" in *The End of Liberalism* (2nd ed., 1979). He uses this term to refer to a perversion of pluralism because of the dominance various private interests maintain in public policymaking. He alludes to the "parceling out to private interests the power to make public policy."

Interest groups are at the center of policymaking. They are essentially self-serving rather than serving the interests of the general public. In deference to interest group demands, government agencies proliferate, regulations expand, and programs multiply. A practical example is the Rural Electrification Administration (REA), which delivers services to rural electrical and telephone utilities in the form of loans or grants; the Environmental Protection Agency (EPA), though requiring more stringent controls on air polluting industries, allows them tax write-offs when buying the necessary pollution equipment, and legislation aimed at reducing the consumption of tobacco can also subsidize tobacco farmers for lost revenues.

Over time, these established relationships become what Lowi calls "iron triangles" or subgovernments (Fig. 2.1). These entities are composed of interest group spokespeople, congressional personnel, and administrators. Under these circumstances, policymaking involves a relatively small number

FIGURE 2.1   Lowi's Iron Triangle

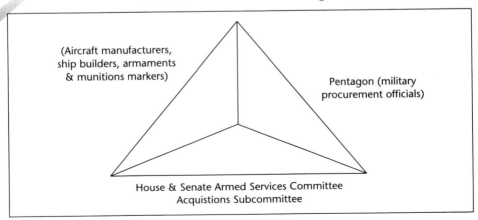

of participants having an internal consensus and a virtual monopoly of information with respect to the issue at hand.

For purposes of clarity and brevity, the antipluralists and their critiques are presented in Table 2.2 on page 18.[7]

As a result of the foregoing, democratic government does not function as assumed by the Founding Fathers. According to Lowi, "the people" are shut out of national agenda setting and policymaking by entrenched, private interests, namely, interest groups. A kind of political Darwinism has taken hold, and the better organized and longer established interests are the dominant forces in today's policymaking.

Schattschneider argues that despite the positive contributions of interest groups offered by both Bentley and Truman, the majority of Americans do not have any interest group representation. He notes, "the flaw in pluralist heaven is that the heavenly chorus sings with a strong upper-class voice." Those who are well-off join political interest groups and strengthen democracy, but the political system is not skewed in favor of one class such as the rich.

While not deploring the existence and political activism of groups (believing the right of association is crucial in a free society), he takes issue with notions that parties are "mere aggregators" of interests. Actually, parties and interest groups consist of different syntheses of interests. Political parties, in contrast to interest groups, appeal to general interests and tend to promote accommodation and compromise among competing interests. The fact that interest groups indulge in lobbying and pursue selected policies distorts the processes of representation. For Schattschneider, this short-circuiting of the majority is undemocratic. A summary of Schattschneider's comparison of parties and interest groups is presented in Box 2.1 on page 19.

Methodologically, a strong challenge to pluralist thought appears in the writings of Mancur Olson, particularly *The Logic of Collective Action* (1965).[8] An economist, Olson argues that Truman does not present a logical empirical theory of interest groups. Olson is especially critical of the idea that interest groups organize whenever there is reason to do so. What is critical are *actual* groups, not *latent* ones. Olson also differentiates between collective incentives for formation and selective incentives. The former give rise to what Olson designates as a "free rider" problem.* In this context, collective goods or goals are often understood to be ideological because they involve reliance on government.

---

*Persons not joining an organization can still gain benefits, (e.g., when one union member gets a raise, all others at that site also get a raise). This is the "free rider" phenomenon. Potential members are unlikely to join an organization because they realize they will receive many of the benefits the group receives regardless of their participation.

TABLE 2.2 The Antipluralist Critiques

Theory	Theorist	Assumption	Critique
Participatory Democracy	Jack Walker (1966) Carole Pateman (1970)	One learns to participate by participating.	Only the minority participates. Pluralism masks a hidden conservative agenda.
Party Government	E. E. Schattschneider (1942, 1966) Sara McCally Morehouse (1981)	Parties are unique custodians of democracy.	Interest groups are inadequate to represent the majority.
Structuralism	Charles Lindblom (1977)	Government depends on business to produce wealth and jobs.	Business groups are privileged.
False Consciousness	William Connolly (1974) Steve Lukes (1974)	Thought and practice are linked. Dominant interests control how interests are conceptualized.	Business class avoids challenge by creating "false consciousness."
Nondecisions	Peter Bachrach and Morton Baratz (1962) Matthew Creson (1971)	Dominant groups prevent issues from being considered.	Pluralism only studies "one face of power."
Interest Group Liberalism	Theodore Lowi (1979)	Bargaining with interest groups creates resistance to change.	Subgovernments dominate discrete policy areas.
Community Power	Dennis Judd (1984)	Economic and social elites use voluntary associations to augment their power.	Private decisions are not decided pluralistically.
Rational Choice	Mancur Olson (1965)	Individuals are rational.	Individuals do not support groups' goals over individual goals.

Source: From Denise L. Baer and David A. Bostis, *Politics and Linkage in a Democratic Society*, (Upper Saddle River, NJ: Prentice Hall, 1993), p. 38.

Selective goods or incentives are available only to those who partici-pate in the group. These incentives can be tangible or intangible. A tangible incentive or benefit can be a hospitalization plan, an insurance policy, or a subscription to a professional journal. Intangible benefits can be satisfac-tion gained from interacting with like-minded persons or feelings of satis-faction gained in working toward the goals of a group.

Finally, Olson rejects the pluralist concept of equilibrium prevailing among groups. Smaller groups are better organized and relatively more cohesive (fewer free rider problems) and are thus able to consistently prevail over large ones. The latter bear greater organizational costs—staffing, inter-nal communications, maintenance, and bargaining to attain consensus—that dissipate resources.

The late Jack Walker's analysis of interest group theory pertained to pluralist concepts of group formation and maintenance. Walker and associ-ates developed a number of new concepts counter to prevailing group the-ories. First, Walker argues that contrary to pluralist doctrines, locating out-side sources of funding takes precedence over membership growth. Second, without sympathetic sponsors or patrons, constituent-based organizations

Box 2.1   Schattschneider's Composition of Political Parties and Interest Groups

Interest Groups	*Political Parties*
Mobilize minorities	Mobilize majorities
Seek only to influence narrow government issues	Makers of government—a bid for power
Irresponsible—lobbying and pressure tactics circumvent popular majorities	Responsible—power depends on persuading a majority of voters
Members share a strong narrow interest and pay dues	Voters have no obligations only rights in the party—not true members
Memberships overlap many other interest groups	Parties are mutually exclusive—cannot be loyal to both parties
Private associations—records are secret	Parties are regulated—finance and voters public
No public test of strength; leaders may exaggerate group membership/support	Periodic public tests of strength in elections

simply do not emerge in any meaningful numbers. With the recent rise of citizen-action organizations (e.g., Common Cause, People for the American Way, or antismoking organizations), older and more traditional patterns of policymaking are being modified. Finally, Walker's research also discovered that material and solidary benefits or inducements are not as significant as assumed by pluralists. Instead, a mixture of purposive and professional benefits are more determinative of group formation.

These critiques offer serious challenges to interest group theory. For example, a pluralist assumption is that policymaking processes and the outcomes they produce are in the general interest of the country. Schattschneider and Lowi suggest they are not. Rather, most public policies have an elitist character.

There is also skepticism that group politics has an inherent self-regulating mechanism. How, then, do antigroup theorists ask: Does this explain the traditional basis in public policymaking with respect to business organizations? Jack Walker's findings undercut Truman's "shared attitudes" as a basis for formation. Rather, it is the political entrepreneur or patron that provides the resources for formation. Finally, the existing divergence among today's political interest groups with respect to size, assets, leadership, political resources, and degree of permanence defies easy classification or categorization. Therefore, antipluralists argue, the universe of groups cannot be easily reduced to a common denominator for theoretical conceptualization.

As shown, antipluralism is the mother of a number of scholars offering a variety of theoretical arguments and perspectives. But, pluralism has its modern proponents such as Austin Ranney, Robert Dahl, and Jeffrey Berry.[9] Nonetheless, a number of strong criticisms remain concerning the inadequate mobilization of majorities, pursuance of narrow goals (especially the so-called single issue groups, e.g., National Rifle Association), and the continuing upper-class bias of the interest group universe. But as later pages demonstrate, interest groups are evolutionary in nature. Many political interest groups quite prominent in the politics of the 1950s and 1960s are less evident today, and the same can be said of what the interest group universe will be in the year 2025.

CHANGES IN GOVERNMENT AND THE INTEREST GROUP GAME

Just as theorizing and conceptualizing the genesis of political interest groups have changed in recent years, so has the political system itself. Most would agree that the size and scope of government at all levels have expanded greatly over the past decades. The consequences both these formal and informal changes raise for political interest groups require further investigation and evaluation.

We already know that initially the national government concerned itself with a limited number of matters—foreign trade, internal improvements such as canals and dams, and national security. Other concerns such as education, welfare, public health, and so on were left to state and local governments. A Frenchman, Alexis de Tocqueville, visiting America in the 1830s, noted that "society governs itself."[10]

Today, the size and shape of federal authority have grown tremendously. Dozens of agencies, bureaus, corporations, and commissions are responding and regulating endless and competing demands of countless individuals and aggregations seeking some kind of benefit for themselves and their members. Modern society has higher expectations of the national government such as the elimination of AIDS, reduction of water and air pollution, and eliminating past imbalances in both public and private employment.

Although aspects of this interaction are discussed more fully later, as the "web" of government expands at all levels, various linkages become established. Farm organizations gravitate to and link with officials having jurisdiction with respect to various farm commodities; veterans and environmental groups are seeking the same kinds of relationships with both national and state regulatory bodies. Each side wants some degree of policy accommodation and stable relationships, although "some are more equal than others" in this context.

Additionally and over time, new advocates emerge as a result of these relationships. Although not planned as such, government policymaking (discussed more fully later in an administrative setting) serves as a catalyst. One needs only to think of the new generation of organized interests with respect to the national government's expansion into environmental regulations as a result of the formation of the Environment Protection Agency. These include Friends of the Earth, the Environmental Defense Fund, and Population Zero.

Also, at one time or another, Washington has actually provided incentives for group establishment. The late Jack Walker notes, for example:

> During the 1960s, the federal government became increasingly active in providing start-up funds to nonprofit sector groups as these groups became less dependent on individuals for seed money. Government agencies have an interest and a well-developed organizational structure and they are often willing supporters of groups in their field.[11]

In addition, given America's heavy worldwide concerns and commitments, many foreign governments have established organizations in the nation's capital that add a further dimension to the interest group universe—American Israel Political Action Committee, Arab American Institute, American Latvian Association, and the Hispanic Policy Development

Project. These and other similar representatives are interested in maintaining various socioeconomic and political ties with the United States that will be beneficial to their respective governments.

Another dimension of expanding government growth and group interaction relates to state and local governments. Recent years have seen a good deal of growth in both the size and scope of state and local governments. This is tied largely to their growing intergovernmental responsibilities with respect to issues like civil rights, welfare, and health. Variously concerned organizations such as the National Governor's Association, National Association of Attorneys General, the National League of Cities, and the Municipal League are heavily involved in dialogue concerning their responsibilities with these and other national social programs. Currently, some thirty states maintain advocacy offices in Washington and in such cities as Los Angeles, Chicago, and New York. The "defunding" policies of the Reagan administration led to increased competition and pressure on the part of these and other organizations for shrinking federal dollars. Nonetheless, one still finds these and other advocacy organizations on the scene today.

Further, various political "entrepreneurs" have appeared on the Washington scene including Ralph Nader, John Gardner, and Ralph Reed. These and others have successfully attracted and retained followers dedicated to their various causes. For them to continue to be influential, they must be articulate and politically knowledgeable. They must also continue to attract affluent donors to replenish their financial coffers and establish important contacts for access and political influence.

The main objective, of course, behind all this group formation and political activism is political access. Interest groups want access and ultimately favorable working relationships with both congressional and executive personnel who have the authority to make decisions that can benefit or hurt interest group concerns. Strategies and actions taken in this regard will vary from group to group and from one policy domain to another.

In some cases, organized interests may seek to "capture" the agency or department that is charged with regulating them. In the process, interest group representatives develop long and friendly relationships with lower level bureaucratic and independent agency personnel that withstand outside pressures for policy change even in the face of significant electoral changes.

In his classic study of regulatory agencies, Marver Bernstein postulates that agencies pass through a series of phases that constitutes a "life cycle."[12] Initially, a new agency is full of enthusiasm and drive to protect the "public interest." As the agency matures, this initial vigor gives way to a kind of "realism" about its role. Finally, in old age, the agency either becomes a protector of the status quo or, worst of all, becomes a captive of the interests it is supposed to serve.

Bernstein points to the Interstate Commerce Commission (ICC); established in 1887, as an example of the latter:

The ICC has become an integral part of the structure of the railroad industry, and its record reflects its commitment to the welfare of that industry ... Increasingly the Commission has identified itself with the interest of the railroad industry ... By failing to exercise administrative initiative, it has permitted private parties to control its flow of work.[13]

What is the situation today? Though capture theories have enjoyed currency among some journalists and scholars, more recent studies raise doubts about their validity.[14] They, indeed, may be too simplistic. Public agencies vary a good deal with respect to structure, their congressional mandates, presidential preferences, popular support, and so on. Additionally, clientele of agencies vary from a few to many and from highly structured organizations to those quite diffuse.[15] Also, agency careerists have their own operating norms and policy perceptions that may not be easily swayed by outside petitioners. Finally, agencies undergo cycles of activism and quiescence. Certainly, for example, the consumer movement and the current activism of antitobacco interests have energized the regulatory activity of the Food and Drug Administration (FDA). The 1990s have witnessed increased regulatory activity on the part of Environmental Protection Agency.[16] Capture theories simply do not provide sufficient data and appreciation of interest group–agency interactions over time.

TOWARD THE FUTURE

It becomes self-evident, then, that interest groups and government are inextricably linked. Threats or disturbances experienced by one set of interests (a recession) undoubtedly impact others to some degree. Nonetheless, interaction patterns persist over time. Success or failures of this linkage in one decade may not necessarily carry over to the next as in the case of environmental groups. Counterforces can emerge seeking to nullify gains made by one set of interests. Conservative interests organized in the late 1970s and early 1980s to counterbalance the gains of liberal environmental groups in the late 1960s and early 1970s. Change is the name of the game. Today's losers may be winners next week or next year.

NOTES

1. Arthur Bentley, *The Process of Government* (Chicago: University of Chicago Press, 1908).
2. Arthur Bentley, *The Process of Government* (San Antonio, TX: Principal Press, 1946), p. 210.

3. Ibid., p. 415.
4. David Truman, *The Governmental Process* (New York: Alfred A. Knopf, 1951).
5. Ibid., p. 14.
6. Robert Dahl, *Who Governs? Democracy and Power in an American City* (New Haven, CT: Yale University Press, 1961), p. 93.
7. Jack Walker, "A Critique of the Elitist Theory of Democracy." *APSR* 60(1966) 285-95; Carole Pateman, *Political Participation and Democracy* (Cambridge, UK: Cambridge University Press, 1970); E. E. Schattschneider, *Party Government* (New York: Farrar and Rinehart, 1942); *Semi-Sovereign People* (New York: Holt, Rinehart and Winston, 1981); Sara McCally Morehouse, *State Politics, Parties, and Policy,* (New York: Holt, Rinehart and Winston, 1981); Charles Lindblom, *Politics and Markets* (New York: Basic Books, 1977); W. E. Connally, *Terms of Political Discourse* (Lexington, MA: D. C. Heath, 1974); Steven Lukes, *Power: A Radical View* (London: Macmillan, 1974); S. Bachrach and Morton Baratz, "Two Faces of Power," *APSR* 56 (1962), pp. 947-52.
8. Mancur Olson, *The Logic of Collective Action* (Boston: Harvard University Press, 1965).
9. Austin Ranney, *Governing: An Introduction to Political Science* (Upper Saddle River, NJ: Prentice Hall, 1990); Robert Dahl, *Who Governs? Democracy and Power in an American City,* 2nd ed. (New Haven, CT: Yale University Press, 1961); Jeffrey Berry, *The Interest Group Society,* 3rd ed. (New York: Longman, 1997).
10. Alexis de Tocqueville, *Democracy in America,* Vols. I and II (New York: Colonial Press, 1899).
11. Jack Walker, *Mobilizing Interest Groups in America: Parties, Professional, and Social Movements* (Ann Arbor: University of Michigan Press), p. 80.
12. Marver Bernstein, *Regulating Business by Independent Commission* (Princeton, NJ: Princeton University Press, 1955).
13. Ibid., pp. 90-91.
14. An example of another captured agency is the former Civil Aeronautics Board (CAB). For a discussion of this, see R. G. Noll and B. M. Owen, *The Political Economy of Deregulation: Interest Groups in the Regulatory Process* (Washington, DC: American Enterprise Institute, 1983).
15. See John E. Chubb, *Interest Groups and the Bureaucracy: The Politics of Energy* (Stanford, CA: Stanford University Press, 1983).
16. For an evaluation of the EPA's role in recent environmental policy making, see Walter A. Rosenbaum, *Environmental Politics and Policy,* 3rd ed. (Washington, DC: CQ Press, 1995).

3

Forces and Actors in Pluralist Politics

The List Is Long and Varied

INTRODUCTION

Thousands of today's citizens view joining groups to influence government policy as an almost sacred right and effective political strategy. As one's friends and neighbors organize, others do so in self-defense. Certainly, the constitutional guarantees of free speech, freedom of expression, and freedom of association legitimize the right to organize and petition government.

Not all citizens, though, are easily organized. Citizens with generally higher socioeconomic status—college educated, upper incomes, prestigiously employed, and high political efficacy—are associated with greater political participation. These individuals believe that the organization maximizes their opportunities to influence public policies most salient to them. Those at the other end of the socioeconomic scale tend to place a higher priority on their economic well-being (e.g., job security).

MOTIVATIONS FOR JOINING

As noted earlier, various rationales exist as to why interest groups emerge and join the political game. Much of the time, organizational affiliations can obtain benefits not generally available to unaffiliated individuals. Political groups tailor their benefits to both attract and retain members. Generally speaking, three types of benefits exist: tangible, solidarity, and purposive.

For the most part, the majority of tangible benefits bestowed by group players are economic. All players, particularly business and labor-oriented organizations, are greatly concerned with the economic well-being of their members. So by affiliating with some organization, the potential member stands to benefit in some way. A labor union, for example, may offer potential members a broader health insurance plan or periodic pay increases not available to nonmembers. The American Farm Bureau Federation offers its members cheaper home heating fuels and less expensive life insurance. The American Medical Association (AMA) offers doctors various stipends to practice

FIGURE 3.1
Organizational Involvement of Demographic Groups: Percentage of Those Involved in an Organization that Takes Stands on Political Issues

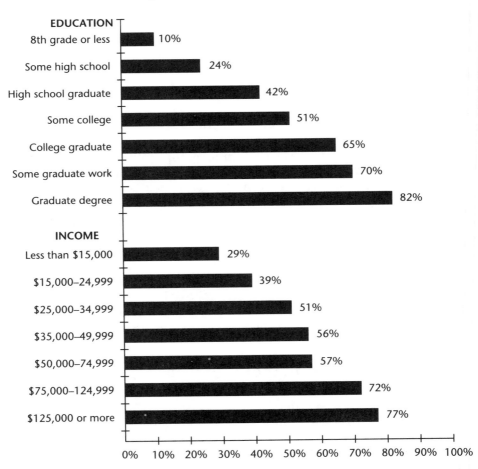

Source: Kay L. Schlozman, "Voluntary Organizations in Politics: Who Gets Involved?" in William Crotty, Mildred A. Schwartz, and John C. Green, eds., *Representing Interests and Interest Group Representation* (Lanham, MD: University Press of America, 1991), p. 76.

in certain locales and hospitals. These types of incentives can be strong inducements for affiliation.

Solidarity benefits naturally result from emotional ties across the membership. Interest group experiences can contribute to greater self-esteem and self-respect. Involvement in some kind of legislative victory or policy change can provide members with a sense of accomplishment or gratification. Members of the AFL-CIO, Common Cause, and Concerned Women of America felt a sense of accomplishment and satisfaction when the Senate rejected the appointment of Robert Bork to the Supreme Court. These organizations, along with other liberal interest groups, lobbied the Senate Judiciary Committee in opposition to Bork. The National Organization for Women offers an emotional refuge for thousands of women who see themselves as second-class citizens in the workplace because of lower salaries, sexual harassment, and limited promotional opportunities.

Purposive benefits are also intangible benefits that derive from having contributed to a worthy cause such as eliminating government waste, fighting industrial pollution, or opposing racial discrimination. These benefits flow from government because some kind of positive action is taken—asserting affirmative action guidelines, government fines levied against polluters, or reducing wanton exploitation of the nation's natural resources. Certainly with respect to the latter, members of the Sierra Club, Friends of the Earth, and the Wilderness Society gain satisfaction in this context as a result of their affiliation.

These benefits are not mutually exclusive. A labor unit, for example, may obtain expanded healthcare for its members and at the same time the members can feel a sense of accomplishment as a result. It must also be kept in mind that interest groups constantly tailor their benefits to attract and retain members. Initially, people were attracted to Common Cause because of its opposition to the Vietnam war. Because of the Watergate scandal, the organization broadened its objectives to include more openness in the processes of government and public funding of both presidential and congressional elections. In doing so, Common Cause has successfully expanded its membership base over time.

Let us now turn to a brief overview and examination of group players presently organized and active in national politics. These are classified both as *economic* or *noneconomic* and according to goal orientation in Box 3.1 on page 28.

AGRICULTURE

American farmers were among the first to become organizational players with the establishment of the national Grange in the 1870s. Common concerns with respect to farm income, commodity production levels, and

BOX 3.1 An Interest Group Typology

Economic

Agriculture

Allied Farm Bureau Federation
Allied Grape Growers
Archer-Daniels-Midland
National Cattlemen's Association
National Cotton Council
National Farmers Union
Tobacco Institute

Business

Bethlehem Steel Corporation
Caterpillar Incorporated
Federal Express
General Motors Corporation
Nationwide Insurance Company
R.J.R. Nabisco
Wal-Mart Stores Incorporated

Labor

AFL-CIO
International Union of Bricklayers
   and Allied Craftsmen
National Education Association
Teamsters
Transportation and Communication
   International Union
United Mine Workers
United Steel Workers of America

Professional

American Association of University
   Professors
American Bar Association
American Dental Association
American Medical Association
Association of Trial Lawyers
   of America
International Union of Operating
   Engineers
Public Securities Association

Noneconomic

Civil Rights

American Arab Anti-Discrimination
   Committee
Anti-Defamation League of B'nai B'rith
Human Rights Campaign Fund
National Association for the Advance-
   ment of Colored People
National Council of La Raza
National Organization for Women

Government

American Federation of Government
   Employees
American Federation of State, County,
   and Municipal Employees
National Association of Counties
National Association of Letter Carriers
National Governors Association
National League of Cities
National Treasury Employees Union

Ideological

American Civil Liberties Union
American Conservative Union
Americans for Democratic Action
Cato Institute
Competitive Enterprise Institute
Conservative Victory Committee

Public Interest

Center for the Study of Responsive Law
Citizens for Tax Justice
Common Cause
Consumer Federation of America
League of Women Voters
Public Citizens
Public Safety Research Institute

Single-Issue

Handgun Control Incorporated
National Abortion Rights Action League
National Rifle Association
National Right to Life Committee
Mothers Against Drunk Driving
Population Zero

producer–processor relationships were contributing factors. Emerging somewhat later were the American Farm Bureau Federation (AFBF) and the
National Corn Growers Association. These and other emerging farm groups
were conduits for channeling farmer discontent to national policymakers,
especially members of Congress. As a result, these early agricultural groups
were successful in the early decades of the twentieth century in transmit-
ting their members' needs and wants. These actions were ultimately successful in gaining favorable farm legislation during and after Franklin Roosevelt's New Deal.

Today interests are quite different. There are currently fewer farm families (about 2 percent of the total population), the family farm is being
replaced by "agribusiness" (large corporate farms), and greater diversity
exists among farm-oriented interests. These do not speak with a united
voice—big farmers versus small ones, grain farmers versus dairy farmers,
livestock producers versus tobacco producers. Furthermore, the food sector
of farming is only one segment; other interests are exporters, Wall Street
traders, food service industries, farm implement dealers, pesticide/fertiliz-
ers manufacturers, and countless others. Under these conditions, drafting
farm legislation is exceedingly difficult.

Additionally, the locus of farm policy has shifted. It is no longer concentrated in the traditional House and Senate agriculture committees and in
the Department of Agriculture. It now spills over to include environmental interests along with those dealing with immigration and energy. Small
wonder that Congress drafts a significant farm bill every 5 years.

In light of the foregoing, a plethora of farm-interests organizations
currently exists. Some of these are listed in Box 3.2[1].

BOX 3.2 A Topology of Contemporary Farm Organizations

Multipurpose Organizations	*Single-Project Organizations*
American Farm Bureau Federation	Agriculture Research Institute
American Seed Trade Association	Environmental Policy Institute
National Cotton Council Processors	Farmers for Fairness
National Farmers' Union	Foundation on Economic Trends
Single-Issue Organizations	*Protest Organizations*
American Farmland Trust	American Agriculture Movement
National Food Processors	Family Farm Movement
National Peanut Growers Group	National Catholic Rural Life Conference
National Soybean Association	North American Farmers' Alliance

As the name implies, multipurpose farm organizations have a range of concerns as well as diverse memberships and broader political contacts. In a typical year, it is not unusual for these organizations to address numerous issues such as agricultural finances, commodity price supports, governmental pesticide controls, and worker-safety laws. Spokespersons for these players maintain contacts with various policymakers in order to remain active players. Staffs of these organizations frequently participate in both agenda setting and policy implementation. They also inform the membership with respect to pending policy shifts. Various media are utilized to accomplish these ends, including newsletters, flyers, workshops, and seminars.

Due to their relatively broad and long-term agricultural concerns, multipurpose organizations range across the political spectrum from conservative to liberal and are so perceived by both legislative and executive personnel. The Farm Bureau takes the relatively more conservative position, whereas the National Farmers' Union (NFU) is more liberal. These perceptions, however, may become modified on such issues as world trade, the disposition of farm surpluses, and the phasing out of certain commodity price supports by Washington. Given the generally reactive and pragmatic responses of these players, the memberships gain a stable and consistent political position that usually coincides with the players' purposes and strategies.

An example of an agricultural protest organization is the American Agriculture Movement (AAM).[2] Emerging in the late 1970s, it was comprised mainly of grain farmers in Southwestern and Great Plains states. The economic status of these farmers, at that time, was one of severe depression because of chronically low prices for their commodities—barley, corn, oats, rye, and wheat. Demanding some kind of governmental relief, hundreds of angry protestors descended on Washington in 1979, in a tractorcade. They purposely snarled and disrupted Washington traffic, destroyed property, and dispersed chickens and livestock on the Capitol grounds to demonstrate their plight.

The protestors' radicalism, however, did not prove successful. Neither national legislators nor administrative personnel offered immediate solutions to the protestor's demands. The organization was leaderless with only "spokesmen" and members that were essentially "participants." It was a loosely structured grass-roots organization lacking in any kind of discipline or control over its members. Its boisterous presence and manners turned off many potential sympathizers.

Over the years, through various internal changes and arrangements, the AAM did establish a more centrally structured organization with dues-paying members in more than a dozen states. It has toned down its protest activity and now works within established lobbying procedures. It has a niche as a grass-roots organization for small farmers.

The AAM has survived now for 20 years, longer than many of its detractors believed it would. Its leadership has shown adaptability and skill in obtaining media coverage, for fund raising, and for alliance building. The organization faces serious challenges in the years ahead as Congress considers cutbacks in farm subsidies and there is growing support for getting "big government" out of the business of financially propping up various sectors of the economy. In the face of continuing uncertainties, many former AAM members have left the business of farming altogether.

The American Farmland Trust (AFT) is relatively new in agricultural organizational politics. As a single-issue organization, it preaches stewardship and conservation of the nation's farmland every year to commercial developers and encourages controlling erosion. To prevent further losses, the AFT solicits donations nationwide to purchase available farmland and lock it away forever from developers.

These donations also fund a long-range and sophisticated educational program aimed at protecting America's farmland beyond the year 2000. AFT personnel interact with national, state, and local actors with respect to public policies and issues affecting the use of existing farmland: land-use planning, sustainable agriculture, public land management, soil erosion controls, wetlands protection, and water quality and resource management.

Additionally, the AFT produces scientifically based studies denoting the costs to American taxpayers in farmland losses and what savings can be gained by preserving it. Finally, the organization provides ongoing technical assistance and expertise to existing local land trusts—there are about 1000 of these throughout the country—aimed at helping these trusts protect and preserve this precious natural resource. Staff personnel offer their special expertise to local planning boards and testify when given the opportunity. Periodic workshops and seminars are held for local farmers aimed at encouraging them to protect their lands through the use of tax-deductible conservation easements (i.e., lands put in trust).

The AFT periodically polls its donors with respect to defining its position on farmland conservation. This information is also transmitted to congressional committees. In the mid-1980s, the AFT, in coalition with the National Farmers' Union and the National Farmers' Organization (NFO), lobbied successfully for several pieces of farm legislation: a conservation reserve to retire highly erodible or environmentally threatened land; the sodbuster and swapbuster provision that disqualified farmers from commodity price support programs if they converted environmentally fragile areas or wetlands to crop production after 1985; and disqualification of those who farmed highly erodible lands without the approval of Soil Conservation Service plans.

Single-project organizations, like the aforementioned single-issue interests, have relatively well-defined goals and immediate concerns. The Foundation on Economic Trends devotes much of its attention to biotechnology and genetic engineering as they relate to farming. Of particular interest has been the development and use of genetically engineered seeds as an alternative to naturally produced seeds. The foundation and its allies see their roles as both informing and educating today's farmers about the potential environmental damage and food shortages if too much reliance is placed on genetically produced seeds in the future.

BUSINESS

Just as agricultural interests emerged at the end of the nineteenth century, so did various business interests begin to organize early in the twentieth century. The Chamber of Commerce of the United States was established in 1912. A conspicuous voice for business, it is a federation of various state and local chambers of commerce, trade associations, and societies of businesspeople. Its major function over the years has been to speak on behalf of its members on issues in public policy such as taxation, foreign imports, wage and price controls, and so on. The chamber is wholeheartedly committed to the American free enterprise system and opposes further expansion of the welfare state.

A more contemporary player for business is the Business Roundtable. Established in the early 1970s, the Roundtable was established:

> to reflect the reallocation of business, human and material resources to political action, new alliances, and structures for coordination; [and] the rapid integration of the emerging new information storage, retrieval, and communication technologies in the service of corporate business political advocacy.[3]

The Roundtable's organizers believed that the concerns of business were not being adequately met by older, more traditional organizations like the chamber and its cohort, the American Association of Manufacturers. These were viewed as too "knee-jerk" reactionary in both their style and rhetoric.

The Roundtable is comprised of chief executive officers (CEOs) of a number of *Fortune Magazine's* 500 corporations. Given the corporate prestige and economic clout of its memberships, it was generally assumed that the organization would establish and maintain an authoritative voice in Washington policymaking as far as business was concerned. This, however, has not proven to be the case as Box 3.3 illustrates. The Roundtable has fallen on bad times and does not have the political influence of some of its peers.

BOX 3.3   *The Fallen Giant* (Jeffrey Birnbaum)

A gang of new Republicans has stomped on the Business Roundtable.

When it was founded 25 years ago, the Business Roundtable was the biggest and baddest lobbying group in Washington. Its 200 chief executives formed the Green Berets of business influence. In the 1970s, when the Roundtable helped defeat a slew of pro-labor laws, its leaders were both industry giants and wily denizens of D.C., such as Irving Shapiro of Du Pont, Reginald Jones of General Electric, John Harper of Alcoa, and Roger Blough of U.S. Steel.

That was then. Now the Roundtable is an also-ran in the rapidly changing world of Washington persuasion. Once a shoo-in for a top-ten slot in any survey of clout in the capital, the Roundtable didn't break into the upper 30 in FORTUNE's recent poll. At No. 33, it was outranked by the likes of the American Trucking Associations and the National Retail Federation. More than 40% of its members are in the lower 250 of the FORTUNE 500, and some of today's most influential companies, like Microsoft and Intel, don't even belong.

The Roundtable is like a vacuum-tube operation struggling to survive in a digital age. When it began, the Roundtable's powerful CEOs could walk into a few key offices at the White House and the Capitol and fix almost any problem. But the demise of Congress' seniority system, the decline of political parties, and the rise of political-action committees have converted once sheeplike members of Congress into independent contractors. A smattering of chief executives can't gather enough votes to do much of anything.

Furthermore, most CEOs are too busy restructuring, reengineering, merging, or acquiring to dabble in public policy. As a result, the Roundtable limits its major initiatives to roughly two a year. It lobbied in favor of a balanced budget in 1995 and for fast-track trade authority this year. But more often the positions it takes are pabulum because of lack of consensus among its diverse membership. On global warming, for instance, the Roundtable merely admonished the President "not to rush to policy commitments." In Washington these days, real players choose sides.

The Roundtable still has one valuable asset: access to cash. But even here, its members divide their giving in a cautiously corporate fashion. Sometimes the funds flow, say, 60% to Republicans and 40% to Democrats-except when it's 60/40 the other way. Such lack of loyalty so incensed GOP leaders that they confronted Roundtable CEOs at a fiery Capitol Hill meeting not long after the 1996 congressional elections. How, in the face of huge spending by the AFL-CIO, could the Roundtable have failed to back the Republicans? Answer: The Roundtable has no control over its members' donations. Complains Ed Gillespie, a former top GOP aide: "They're a wasted resource and just plain irrelevant."

In contrast, the new elite of business lobbies is decidedly Republican. The so-called GOP Gang of Five includes old standbys like the National Association of Manufacturers (No. 13) and the Chamber of Commerce of the

U.S.A. (No. 15). But the ringleaders are hyperactive upstarts such as the National Federation of Independent Business (No. 4), the National Restaurant Association (No. 24), and the National Association of Wholesaler-Distributors (No. 47 overall, but No. 28 among Republicans).

What these groups have in common is that despite the occasional dalliance with Democrats, especially by the broad-membership Chamber and the NAM, they were unmistakably Republican before being Republican was cool. Now, with the pro-business party firmly in control of Congress, the Gang forms the core of two of the GOP's most secretive and influential inner sanctums: the Thursday Group, which lobbies at the behest of Republican congressional leaders, and the Coalition, which raises millions to help elect GOP lawmakers. The Gang of Five's far-flung members can be counted on to press for almost any Republican cause. "These groups were with us when we were in the wilderness," says Ohio Congressman John Boehner, the Fourth-ranking GOPer in the House. "And they're still with us now."

Source: Fortune Magazine, December 8, 1997, pp. 156-157.

ORGANIZED LABOR

The extensive industrialization and commercialization of the nation during the latter quarter of the nineteenth and early twentieth centuries motivated workers' desires and concerns for some kind of industry organization to represent them. Growing concerns with wages, grievance procedures, and working conditions contributed to unionization.

Today, the AFL-CIO, with approximately 13 million members, represents about 100 different unions. It is the most authoritative voice for organization labor. Corresponding to many large corporations, the federation encompasses a wide variety of occupations—teachers, sanitation workers, steel workers, electricians, plumbers, chemical workers, auto workers, plus thousands of workers at the state and municipal levels. The AFL-CIO maintains a large professional staff in Washington for purposes of disseminating information to members and lobbying. AFL-CIO lobbyists are some of the most numerous on Capitol Hill. One of their key targets on the Hill is the Education and Labor Committee of the House of Representatives. Linkages are also maintained with such bureaucrats as Health and Human Services, Labor, and Department of Education personnel.

Although American labor unions have primarily been concerned with economic benefits—wages, fringe benefits, retirement systems, profit sharing, and working conditions—their concerns have broadened to include such issues as welfare reform, job training, consumer protection, civil rights, and tax reform. It is not unusual to see individual affiliated unions pursue their own unique concerns through political action.

An important strategy as a political player has been labor's work within the Democratic party. The federation's resources and manpower have consistently gone to elect Democratic presidents and members of Congress. The federation's Committee on Political Education (COPE) was the first political action committee to endorse and fund party campaigns that also included such activities as disseminating campaign literature, establishing phone banks, and participating in get-out-the-vote drives on election day.

With respect to lobbying, its representatives saturate Capitol Hill when needed. The federation supports about 300 lobbyists working with about fifty affiliated unions found in all fifty states and congressional districts. These can be quickly activated when issues crucial to labor (e.g., minimum wage legislation) are before the Congress.

Labor's political clout today is totally different from what it was during the late 1940s and early 1950s. First, there is the problem of declining membership. As Figure 3.2 on page 36 shows, only about 15 percent of today's work force is unionized. With fewer workers joining unions, their political base is eroding. This translates into reduced political influence. Second, labor's image remains tarnished because of a closed, autocratic system of governance contaminated by past experiences in corruption and racketeering within its leadership, Jimmy Hoffa, Dave Beck, and Larry Presser being prime examples. Further, labor's image was not helped by its relatively late push for equal rights for minority workers and women during the 1960s and 1970s. In short, a general malaise has prevailed within union ranks and the leadership with respect to direction and purpose.

But a change in political fortune may be in the wind. John J. Sweeney, an insurgent candidate, was swept into office in the fall of 1995. In a sharp break with its past complacency, the AFL-CIO under Sweeney is embarking on an ambitious, coordinated action plan to reverse labor's political fortunes. In 1996, it spent $35 million to mobilize the membership and launch an advertising blitz. In the gloomy aftermath of a dozen years of Republican presidencies and the 1994 Republican takeover of Congress, federation leaders realize that they must be much better organized and active in their efforts to elect Democratic supporters. If this is accomplished, labor can reestablish itself as a force within the Democratic party. In an era of growing public distrust with policies and mistrust of established institutions, it is simply not enough to endorse and attend candidate fund-raisers.

At the grass-roots level, the federation is initiating a series of "town hall" meetings to elicit testimonials from its members that highlight issues of stagnating wages and the income gap. Presentations include examples of employers with poor records on layoffs, working conditions, and employee benefits. Affiliated unions are also working to get measures on various state ballots that raise minimum wage issues and improve turnout among union members and other working-class voters.[4]

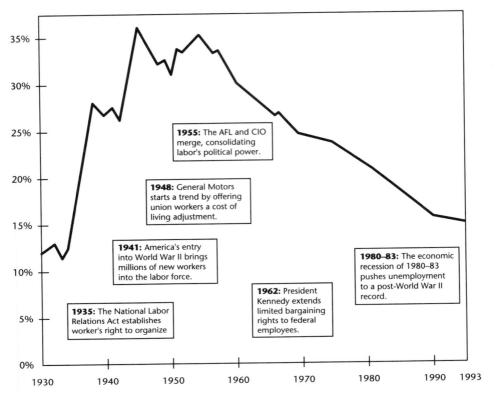

FIGURE 3.2
Percentage of Wage and Salary Workers Who are Union Members

PROFESSIONALS

A leading voice and player on behalf of the American medical profession and doctors is the American Medical Association (AMA). In fact, this association affects the lives of millions of Americans in a subtle fashion. A family doctor's training as medical student and then as resident is influenced by standards the AMA established. In addition, the AMA has a hand in the continuing education that maintains doctors' skills and knowledge after they are in practice. Furthermore, the AMA's principles of medical ethics and opinions from the association's Council of Ethical and Judicial Affairs guide doctors' behavior with their patients.

In the eyes of most citizens and many politicians, the AMA is the premier practitioner of medical arts and medical politics. It is literally an 800-

pound gorilla on Capitol Hill. No other player involved with healthcare—and certainly no consumer organizations—can match the AMA in terms of political access or influence to national politicians. It consistently outspends not only all other medical groups in lobbying but many other types of groups as well. (In recent election cycles, the AMA has consistently contributed over $3 million to various political candidates.) Past presidents like Franklin Roosevelt and Harry Truman sought modest changes in the healthcare system without checking with the association and found themselves stymied. It has great influence as a legislative spoiler, delayer, or even derailer of the best-laid plans of presidents and consumer activists. President Clinton and his wife found their plans for changes in the healthcare system largely blocked by the association's political allies.

Although the AMA claims to represent 90 percent of the nation's doctors, this is somewhat overblown. Historically, the association has proclaimed itself as the "voice of medicine." It is a catchy phrase that harks back to the 1950s and 1960s. But with congressional enactment of Medicare and Medicaid, rising dues, and infighting within the membership over abortion rights, the association's membership is not what it used to be. A closer examination of figures shows a membership of about 300,000. According to one source, membership was about 275,000 in 1993. This source goes on to say:

> the AMA doctors its figures. Subtract 32,045 medical students ... the membership falls to 243,465, and market share dips to 38 percent physicians. Eliminate all physicians with reduced dues, such as residents, young physicians and military doctors and also dues-exempt retirees, and you are left with 153,268 members, just 24 percent of American doctors, who pay full annual dues of $420.[5]

Thus, the proportion of full-dues paying members is less than half of what it was 20 years ago and only about a third of what is was in the 1960s.

The AMA is organized somewhat along the lines of our federal and state governments. At the center of things is the house of delegates, its legislative branch. It is comprised of delegates from all fifty states and U.S. territories. Delegates are elected by state or territorial societies rather than by popular vote. Various specialty groups within the membership—surgeons, pediatricians, gynecologists—make up the largest membership block. Other delegates are selected by medical staffs, medical schools, students, and military physicians. Each specialty group has one vote, and the total is 440.

The house of delegates meets twice a year to vote on hundreds of resolutions and reports prepared by the AMA's board of trustees, various councils, and committees. These deal with such topics as medical ethics, public health, the delivery of medical services, and medical education. Positions taken at these meetings serve as AMA policy and help guide its 1200-member staff on what direction to take in its day-to-day activities. These policy decisions are not legally binding but have influenced state and federal policymakers and courts.

One of the more important duties of the house of delegates is to elect the AMA's important board of trustees, which is sort of an executive branch along with the president. This board has the ultimate legal and financial responsibility for the association. It has an annual budget of about $180 million and also has investments and owns stocks, real estate, and other businesses.[6] The trustees frequently fly to Washington to inform executive and legislative personnel of AMA policies. They also appear before various state and local subsidiaries and hear their concerns. The whole board meets every other month. The real power rests with the chairperson who decides who will do what in the coming months. Persons holding this position may very well be in line to become association president.

The house of delegates is not truly representative of the association's membership. Most delegates are older and more established doctors with more time to devote to medical politics. The typical delegate today is an office-based private physician at a time when more doctors are working for hospitals, health maintenance organizations, or in other nontraditional settings. The AMA does have student, resident, and young physician sections, but these generally are not represented in the hierarchy of the organization. As a result, the house of delegates underrepresents today's younger, more ethnically and racially diverse groups and the growing number of women doctors. The average delegate, then, is a white male, approximately 63 years old, whereas the average age of today's doctors is 45.

The political arm of the association is the American Medical Association Political Action Committee (AMPAC). This is a conduit through which the association collects and funnels its contributions to friendly politicians. AMPAC operates independently of the association, but there is overlap in doctors who move back and forth from AMPAC to the board of trustees. AMPAC has gained a good deal of notoriety as one of the bigger political action committee (PAC) spenders. The AMA and AMPAC have frequently clashed with various public interest groups like Public Citizen and Common Cause over the association's large contributions. Both public interest groups have consistently called for stricter limits on campaign contributions.

AMPAC funnels its money to officeholders who are in a position to advance its economic concerns and political agenda. Like other organizations, AMPAC contributes to its friends but seeks to punish its enemies. Interestingly, the association has not put its money on the line with respect to such public health issues as gun control, tobacco, or abortion.

Presently, the AMA is locked in a fierce battle over healthcare reform. Early on, the AMA set out to protect the existing system by promoting limited reforms to avert a major restructuring or greater government involvement. The association has declared war on proposals borrowed from the Canadian healthcare "single-player" system. Although acknowledging that there is need for reform, it continues to oppose fundamental changes. The AMA also attacks national systems in other countries by insisting on an "American" solution. In the process, the association has resorted to scare tactics, raising alarms about "rationing" healthcare amid cries of "socialism." The association will continue to use every tactic and spend every dollar it can in this battle. Let the public beware: The AMA is playing for keeps, and its concerns are with doctors, not with patients.

CIVIL RIGHTS

The 1960s and 1970s witnessed the emergence and growth of a new generation of political groups. Coalitions of middle-upper-class professionals and intellectuals emerged in their opposition to the Vietnam war and racial and sexual discrimination. This broad socioeconomic movement was spearheaded by young elements of the upper class for whom those civil rights and antiwar movements came in their formative years, just as the Great Depression and World War II had for their parents.

This consciousness raising not only helped these new players define their political position but served as a motivating force for organizations as well. A uniqueness of this generation of political interest groups was that their goals did not bring immediate member gratification. Rather, what was being sought was a general good—clean air, clean water, greater gender equality, world peace, and so on.

Characteristic of the organizational players at this time is the National Organization for Women. Established in 1966, NOW came into being because millions of women were convinced that an authoritative voice in national policymaking on their behalf was lacking. Despite having won the right to vote in 1919 and the 1964 Civil Rights Act banning discrimination based on sex, many women believed these were not sufficient. Both national and state legislation were needed to redress grievances many women claimed exist in education, employment, pay, and so on. A national lobby needed to be established to sensitize the nation's political institutions—Congress, courts, and state legislatures—on issues related to women.

As a multipurpose organization and player, NOW has been quite conspicuous in recent political battles. It was, for example, deeply involved in the unsuccessful ratification battle over the Equal Rights Amendment (ERA).[7] It not only networked with other feminist organizations like the National Women's Political Caucus (NWPC), the American Association of University Women, and the National Abortion Rights Action League (NARAL), but with other pro-ERA groups as well. A key strategy was to broaden their political base by soliciting the support of church-related organizations (United Methodists) and occupational organizations like the AFL-CIO and its affiliated unions.

As the ERA struggle continued, NOW and its allies not only broadened their political base but undertook a series of strategic actions aimed at final ratification. In this context, NOW and its allies produced a series of pro-ERA documents, drafted and disseminated legal opinions supporting ratification, and indulged in periodic fund-raising to keep the issue before reluctant state legislators. NOW was also prominent in publicizing the infamous "59-cent gap." As of 1980, for every dollar men earned, women earned just 59 cents. Millions of buttons emblazoned with "59 cents" were distributed nationwide, and they were a powerful symbol of existing sex discrimination.

NOW is also a key player in today's abortion politics. A strong supporter of abortion rights, its national officers have testified before congressional committees considering the nationalization of abortion rights. One of its former presidents, Eleanor Smeal, was heavily involved in the 1992 presidential campaign in behalf of the pro-choice Clinton–Gore ticket. Ms. Smeal and others in the leadership frequently call upon their members at the state and local levels to indulge in fund-raising and political activism so as to defeat pro-life candidates and replace them with pro-choice women. NOW also maintains a Legal Defense and Education Fund. Its purpose is to provide legal assistance to women claiming violations of their constitutional rights, (e.g., sexual harassment, verbal abuse, or the dissemination of pornographic materials in the workplace). The fund also publishes the *Supreme Court Review,* which alerts the national press with respect to litigation concerning women's issues. It is a tool for shaping both public opinion as well as influencing news coverage of issues of importance to millions of women. Finally, the fund also conducts political research with respect to future litigation and trains new women's rights attorneys.

As a key civil rights player, NOW utilizes its resources to influence national policies not only of interest to its supporters but for broader constituencies as well. Similar to other civil rights organizations, NOW utilizes a range of strategies for challenging the political status quo.

IDEOLOGICAL INTEREST ORGANIZATIONS

Another set of important players is idea- or issue-based. They differ from economic interests in that material benefits are not their primary goal. Rather, these players are organized and motivated by a belief system or ideal about how society and government should be structured and what public policies are most desirable. Ideological players are varied and include such organizations as the American Conservative Union, the American Civil Liberties Union, National Gay Rights Organization, and the Cato Institute.

The Cato Institute, like most of the aforementioned organizations, is organized around a set of social and political ideas. It can also be perceived as an expressive organization; it reaches out to the public through the mass media.

Cato is a Washington-based research foundation that was established in 1977. It is named for the *Cato Letters,* libertarian pamphlets disseminated in the American colonies prior to the outbreak of the Revolutionary War. Institute founders claim the *Letters* played a crucial role in laying the philosophical foundation for the American Revolution.

Because of its politically conservative orientation, Cato is philosophically opposed to the "bewildering array of governmental programs aimed at combating hunger, poverty, unemployment, and other social programs." Not only do these and similar programs fail to alleviate these conditions, but they waste billions of taxpayers' dollars in the process. In addition, Cato argues, the national government has become so pervasive that it stifles individual liberties and interferes with the proper functioning of a free economy. What is needed to correct these conditions is a renaissance of our "original" ideas on personal freedom, peace, and humanity. If this rebirth is successful, the nation would be better able to deal with the crucial issues it faces daily.

Many of Cato's activities are in public policy research. It has more than 1200 sponsors and over 500 subscribers to its publications. These are designed to initiate and stimulate public debate and assist the layperson in choosing the most rational alternative with respect to socioeconomic policies. Cato also publishes several dozen books a year on a wide range of issues such as agriculture, energy use, judicial philosophy, the privatization of the nation's oil and gas industries, U.S. involvement abroad, and so on. Numerous monographs and journals are also available and aimed at alerting public officials to Cato's positions on issues. Staff members, as well as sympathetic supporters in various college and university faculties, contribute to the publications.

A brief analysis shows the following:

Founded: 1977.

Purpose: "The Cato Institute is a public policy research foundation dedicated to broadening the parameters of policy debate to allow consideration of more options that are consistent with the traditional American principles of limited government, individual liberty, and peace. To that end, the Institute strives to achieve greater involvement of the intelligent, concerned lay public in questions of policy and the proper role of government."

Policy Areas: Agriculture; crime and criminal justice; defense and foreign affairs; economics, business and labor; education; electoral and governmental reform; energy and environment; health, welfare and poverty; housing and land use; science and technology; transportation.

Research Priorities: Consistent with policy areas.

Operating Methods: Research; publications; conferences and seminars; media outreach; legislative testimony; library or information clearinghouse.

Budget Category: $5,000,001 to $10,000,000.

Funding Sources: Corporations, 12 percent; corporate and private foundations (the Institute combines these two categories), 30 percent; publication sales, conferences, etc., 8 percent; individuals, 50 percent.

Publications: Periodicals—*The Cato Journal* (three times a year journal); *Cato Policy Report* (bimonthly newsletter); *Regulation* (quarterly magazine); *Foreign Policy Briefing* (report series); *Policy Analysis* (report series); *Briefing Papers* (report series); *Annual Report.* Books and Reports—*The Last Monopoly: Privatizing the Postal Service for the Information Age* (1996); *Affirmative Action Fraud* (1996); *Oil, Gas, and Government* (1996); *Economic Freedom of the World: 1975–1995* (1996); *Money and Markets in the Americas* (1996); *Educational Freedom in Eastern Europe* (1995); *The Government Factor: Undermining Journalistic Ethics in the Information Age* (1995); *Science Without Sense: The Risky Business of Public Health Research* (1995); *The Captive Press: Foreign Policy Crises and the First Amendment* (1995). Op-Ed Articles— 444 articles.

Library: Maintains library of 3000 books and 130 periodicals concerning economics, political philosophy, history, and political science.

Staff: Seventeen full-time research; twenty full-time support; one part-time support.

Organizational Structure: Independent.

PUBLIC INTEREST GROUPS

A relatively new constellation of interests emerged in the latter part of the 1960s and in 1970s. These claim to speak for broad and varied classes of citizens—consumers, disenchanted voters, environmentalists, and political reformers. These organizations perceive themselves as anti-status quo and representing the public interest as opposed to the narrow "selfish" interests of business, trade unions, and other "special" groups. The purposes of these public interest groups are more broadly based and not essentially self-serving. They include more government regulation of business and its products, campaign finance, and improving conditions in the workplace. These activists are responsible for congressional enactment of environmental, occupational, and health legislation and consumer protection laws.

Citizens for Tax Justice (CTJ) is concerned with reforming the income tax code in favor of lower income citizens. It was established in response to California's passage of Proposition 13 (1978), which drastically cut that state's residential and commercial taxes and a number of public services. The primary purpose of CTJ is to give ordinary citizens a voice and more influence in the formulation of tax legislation at all levels of government. It is especially concerned with the level of taxation borne by low- and middle-income families across the nation. CTJ takes the position that there should be some equitable correlation between one's income and the amount of tax one pays.

The organization's push for reform began in 1984 when its director, Robert McIntyre, a Nader-trained lawyer, and his staff began compiling annual reports of the nation's largest corporations over the period 1981–1984. These data came from the files of the Securities and Exchange Commission (SEC). Over several months, the staff extracted tax data from these reports as well as the amount of annual corporate profits.

In the summer of 1986, CTJ published its findings in a report entitled *130 Reasons We Need Tax Reform*. The report states:

> These 130 companies, ranging from Aetna Life and Casualty to Xerox, earned $72.9 billion in pre-tax domestic profits in the years they did not pay federal income taxes. But instead of paying $33.5 billion in income taxes, as the 46 percent statutory rate purports to require, they received $6.1 billion in tax rebates.[8]

To maximize the effect of these findings, CTJ made them available to the mass media. Almost overnight, newspapers across the country began running stories of "corporate freeloaders," noting companies such as AT&T, Boeing, General Mills, Texaco, and DuPont. The thoroughness and the accuracy of the report left little room for the listed companies to charge bias or claim harassment. The report was based primarily on each company's own figures. These news stories produced a citizen backlash against the high profits of big business and demands for tax reform.

The timing of the report was strategic as its release came at the same time the House and Senate tax-writing committees were in conference considering changes in the existing federal tax code. Numerous copies of the report found their way to the committee members. Various labor unions inundated members of Congress with letters strongly denouncing the 130 businesses for not paying their fair share of taxes and at the same time getting rebates. Although the 1986 tax bill did not go as far as the CTJ wished, in a subsequent publication it was noted:

> There are some problems. ... But tax reform represents a giant step in the direction of fairness: The number of corporate tax avoiders has been greatly reduced, most of the worst offenders of the past decade have begun to pay their fair share.[9]

SINGLE-ISSUE ORGANIZATIONS

Another type of political player is the single-issue organization. Members of these groups have a strong, almost emotional, dedication to their cause—pro-choice versus pro-life, smokers versus nonsmokers, or gun control advocates versus gun owners. Single-issue groups can, at times, be extremely effective when their opposition is diffuse or poorly organized. They can marshal enormous energy and resources in their focus on a single concern.

A highly visible and active player in this regard in national politics today is the National Rifle Association (NRA). Established 1871 by a handful of military officers, its initial purpose was to improve and maintain effective marksmanship in our armed forces. Over the succeeding decades, the association saw its numbers increase, thanks largely to its affiliation with various sporting and hunting clubs throughout the nation. At the end of World War II, an influx of returning soldiers provided a significant boost, almost tripling the membership. Most of these new members, however, were mainly interested in hunting. In the mid-fifties, with a membership over a quarter million and a staff well over a hundred, the NRA moved its national headquarters to Washington, D.C.

In the late 1960s, when Congress turned its attention to gun control, so did the NRA. From that point on, greater emphasis has been placed on the organization's political agenda and more political commentary has appeared in its publication, *American Rifleman,* with more space devoted to legislative issues before the Congress.

This heightened political consciousness led to the establishment of the Institute for Legislative Action (ILA). Focusing primarily on legislative initiatives on the state and national levels, it is a driving force within the NRA. In the 1990s, it has consumed about one quarter of the organizational budget. With respect to its lobbying influence, the *Washington Post* notes, "few lobbies have so mastered the marble halls and concrete canyons for Washington."[10]

Beyond its lobbying responsibilities, the ILA is the catalyst for member mobilization. Through the use of legislative alerts and mass mailings, the rank and file are energized to contact their legislators. These communiqués are frequently cast in politically charged terms to dramatize the importance of the issue at hand. One journalist labels this tactic the "Armageddon appeal."[11] A study of NRA advertising conducted by the Congressional Research Service found numerous inaccuracies in the way the NRA literature describes gun bills before the Congress.

Currently, the NRA maintains its position as the key player with regard to all forms of gun regulation. In doing so, it maintains an ideological purity that both helps and hurts. It helps from the standpoint of being able to mobilize and activate the membership on a moment's notice. It hurts in that it alienates its former allies.* A split has developed over the NRA's opposition to armor-piercing (so-called cop-killer) bullets. This type of ammunition has no sporting or hunting value, unless the quarry is a police officer in a bulletproof vest.

The split widened when local police forces across the nation came out in favor of the Brady Bill, which requires a waiting period for handgun purchases. Additionally, in 1988, the NRA ran advertisements claiming Joseph McNamara, the police chief of San Jose, California, favored legalizing drugs, a charge that proved to be false. Finally, the NRA sought to expel former President George Bush from membership because of his 1989 decision to ban the importation of semiautomatic rifles into the United States. The benefits of compromise are being discarded for continued issue purity.

Although the preceding typology is but a microcosm of the interest group universe, it does provide some helpful insights. For example, it demonstrates both the diversity and the complexity of citizen associations. American politics is increasingly group based. Virtually all segments of society have found it necessary to organize in order to express their concerns or grievances. Additionally, member benefits vary from one organization to another, although some players may offer several types of benefits. In addition, a newer generation of interest players is now on the national scene. This has led to greater political competition between the older players in contrast to the new. The newer players seek benefits that are for broader distribution such as clean air, more open government, or campaign reforms. Implicit in this, then, is that the group universe is dynamic, diverse, and exceedingly aggressive. These characteristics will undoubtedly continue well beyond the year 2000.

---

*The NRA joined the Christian Coalition's efforts to elect more conservative Republicans to the House in both 1994 and 1996.

NOTES

1. See William P. Browne, *Private Interests, Public Policy, and American Agri-culture* (Lawrence: University of Kansas Press, 1988), p. 57.
2. See Allan J. Cigler, "Organizational Maintenance and Political Activity on the 'Cheap': The American Agriculture Movement," in *Interest Group Politics*, 3rd ed., Allan J. Cigler and Burdett A. Loomis, (Washington, D.C.: Congressional Quarterly Press, 1991), pp. 81–105.
3. Michael Pertschuck, *Revolt Against Regulation: The Rise and Pause of the Consumer Movement* (Berkeley: University of California Press, 1982), p. 57.
4. See "Laboring Uphill," *National Journal,* 28 March 2, 1996, pp. 474–478.
5. Harold Wolinsky and Tom Brune, *The Serpent on the Staff: The Unhealthy Politics of the America Medical Association* (New York: Jeremy P. Tarcher/Putnam Books, 1994), p. 6.
6. Ibid., p. 9.
7. On this point, see Jane J. Mansbridge, *Why We Lost the ERA* (Chicago: University of Chicago Press, 1986).
8. Robert S. McIntyre and Jeff Spinner, *130 Reasons Why We Need Tax Reform* (Washington, DC: Citizens for Tax Justice, 1986), p. 2.
9. Robert S. McIntyre, J. M. Crystal, and David C. Wilhelm, *The Corporate Tax Comeback: Corporate Income Taxes After Tax Reform* (Washington, D.C: Citizens for Tax Justice, 1993), p. 2.
10. Quoted in Osha Gray Davidson, *Under Fire: The NRA and the Battle for Gun Control* (New York: Holt, 1993), p. 39.
11. This label was initiated by Osha Gray Davidson, a Washington news journalist.

4

Lobbyists and Lobbying

Key Actors and Strategies in Pursuit of Policy Influence

INTRODUCTION

Effective governmental representation of citizen interests depends, in large part, on the respective spokesperson or lobbyist. According to Al Gore:

> An effective lobbyist should have integrity, knowledge of political issues, and of the climate shaping political debate, a sense of priorities and of where issues fit into other matters of consideration, and the ability to communicate quickly and clearly.[1]

The choice of a lobbyist or organizational spokesperson, of course, is contingent on a number of structural and strategic factors. Certainly, organizational size, level of resources, goals, and strategies must be factored in. Some political interests, for instance, have limited or few political objectives, whereas others have broader and more varied concerns (small businesses are characteristic of the former, and labor unions are frequently characteristic of the latter). Further, some interests require only brief and temporary representation, whereas others open permanent offices in Washington. In some instances, only a political generalist (one with a general knowledge of the workings of the political system) suffices, whereas other associations may require expert or technical representation (requiring a representative with knowledge of the intricacies of corporate tax laws). Finally, expertise in bureaucratic lobbying may be required which may necessitate a choice different from one with extensive time and knowledge of Capitol Hill.

PROFILE OF WASHINGTON REPRESENTATIVES

Several common characteristics of Washington representatives are presented in Box 4.1. Not surprisingly, a disproportionate number are lawyers. Why is this the case? Unlike professionals in other areas (e.g., doctors, engineers, teachers) lawyers' training qualifies them to give advice on proposed legislation or on changes in the law involving a client. In fast-moving legislative sessions, for example, lawyers are best qualified to discuss or rewrite amendments. In addition, lawyers can more easily explain to their client the scope of a bill, the meaning of a section thereof, the present state of existing legislation, and the relationship of pertinent statutes. While nonlawyer representatives can explain the need for certain legislation, lawyer representatives can show how changing the law can meet the client's needs.

One would be wrong, however, to assign too much policy influence to lawyers. A legal education can provide entrée to government service, typically in the executive branch. These individuals, though, are frequently employed as legal counsels of one type or another. And after this kind of experience, they may move on to a private law firm. Legal training, then, is

BOX 4.1 Common Characteristics of Washington Representatives

1. Washington representatives are overwhelmingly white males. Female representatives, while fewer in number, are relatively more visible now, especially in the health field.

2. Washington representatives tend to be middle aged (45–65), of Anglo-Saxon origin, and Protestant. Catholic and Jewish representatives are present but in fewer numbers. They tend to be more numerous in unions and professional organizations.

3. Though publicly proclaiming nonpartisanship, a good number of representatives tilt toward the Democratic party. More Democrats than Republicans look to Washington for all kinds of problem solving. In such policy areas as labor and energy, Democrats prevail, whereas more Republican representatives are involved in business and agriculture.

4. A disproportionate number of representatives come from middle and upper income families with professional backgrounds.

5. The majority of organizational spokespersons have long ties to the District of Columbia area. In order to know the political system and establish meaningful ties and contacts, most representatives have been on the Washington scene for a decade or more.

Note: See John P. Heinz, Edward O. Laumann, Robert L. Nelson, and Robert H. Salisbury, *The Hollow Core: Private Interests in National Policy Making* (Cambridge, MA: Harvard University Press, 1993).

a convenient route to public employment, but it does not necessarily follow that it leads inevitably to policy influence.

The economic conservative liberalism of Washington lobbyists is also relevant. Certainly, early socialization processes condition one's political outlook. Therefore, if a lobbyist's maturation tilts conservatively, this can be an important factor in both recruitment and career choice. In this case, chances are good that lobbyist affiliation will be in the corporate or business association field. Conversely, representatives from liberal families tend to gravitate toward labor unions or citizen action groups. In both cases, ideological selection can be quite strong.

Another factor that conditions lobbying choice and effectiveness is the network of acquaintances a representative interacts with. An old euphemism is that the broader and more varied one's contacts become, the better it is. However, representative patterns demonstrate something more structured. Certainly, any kind of networking can begin with "old school" ties (i.e., friends and former classmates from law or graduate school). Additionally, a network of acquaintances emerges from politics and government, working in congressional or state campaigns or in federal noncongressional experiences that includes agency or bureau employment.

In this context, the workplace is of special importance. It is here that organizational policies, strategies, and responsibilities are worked out. Over time, a process of informal socialization takes place with the representative becoming more fully acquainted with an organization's policy orientations as well as its political interactions with other organizations. The duration and nature of theses relationships vary from one association to another. Among the relatively newer citizen action groups, relationships are much less well-developed. On the other hand, labor unions and Washington-based law firms and business associations are more established and have relatively more permanent networks in place.

The number and variety of lobbyists and lobbying firms have exploded over the past quarter century. Currently, some 19,000 men and women are employed as lobbyists. They are employed by approximately 4000 private corporations, trade associations, labor unions, and other interests as well as by law firms, public relations firms, and consulting institutions. These numbers are constantly changing as new players enter the game, temporarily drop out, and combine or recombine with other associations. The composition of today's forces will undoubtedly be quite different in the year 2005.

COMPONENTS OF THE LOBBYING ESTABLISHMENT

What are the major personnel components of today's lobbying establishment? A highly visible component is former members of Congress. An increasing number of former senators become organizational representatives—Howard Baker, Steven Symms, and Robert Dole. Former House members presently lobbying are Thomas Downey, Norman Lent, Vin Weber, and Guy Vader Jagt. Irrespective of party, the experience and knowledge acquired through congressional experiences are valuable commodities. These and other exmembers offer their clients contacts to congressional leaders that other spokespersons cannot (see Box 4.2).

The same can be said for former members of the executive branch. The experiences and knowledge gained by former White House officials—Ed

BOX 4.2   Ex-GOP Lawmakers Find Second Careers

The Republican takeover of Congress has buoyed the fortunes not only of lobbying shops recently opened by entrepreneurial former GOP Members, but of established K Street operations that include GOP congressional alumni among their partners.

Lobbying practices that are doing particularly well in the current political climate include the Washington office of the Cleveland-based law firm of Arter & Hadden, where former Texas Rep. Tom Loeffler hangs out his shingle; the Washington office of Baker & Hostetler, a Cleveland-based law firm where former Michigan Rep. Guy Vander Jagt is a partner; and the Washington lobbying firm of Downey Chandler Inc., of which former Republican Rep. Rod Chandler of Washington is a name partner.

In interviews, both Loeffler and Chandler said their businesses have grown markedly in recent months. Loeffler, who joined Arter & Hadden in mid-1993, said that the firm's government affairs practice boasts 12 professionals, almost double the number when he started.

Both former lawmakers represent major corporate clients. Chandler has worked for Fuji Photo Film USA, Microsoft Corp. and Time Warner Inc. Loeffler's blue-chip clients include the Edison Electric Institute, Monsanto Co., Sprint Corp. and Westinghouse Electric Corp.

Many Washington lobbying firms find it especially effective—and profitable—to deploy Republican and Democratic former lawmakers in tandem when servicing key accounts. Chandler, for example, was recruited by former Rep. Thomas J. Downey, D-N.Y., who is president of their firm. Loeffler works closely with ex-Rep. Dennis E. Eckart, D-Ohio, a senior partner at Arter & Hadden.

Vander Jagt, who went to work for Baker & Hostetler after losing a reelection bid in 1992, is particularly well positioned to work with the current Congress. After serving in the House for 26 years, Vander Jagt was recruited by a former Capitol Hill protégé, Kenneth J. Kies, who had joined the firm in the late 1980s and built up a lucrative tax practice.

Vander Jagt, who served many years on the House Ways and Means Committee, had earlier played a role in bringing Kies from Baker & Hostetler's Cleveland office to the Ways and Means panel, where he rose to the post of chief minority tax counsel.

Kies has gone through the revolving door again and is back in Congress as chief of staff at the Joint Committee on Taxation, and Vander Jagt has taken over most of his former clients. "I inherited the practice of Ken Kies," a grateful Vander Jagt acknowledged. That business includes several important insurance clients such as Johnson & Higgins, the National Association of Insurance Brokers, and the Travelers Group.

Vander Jagt also credits the Republican takeover of Congress with helping to spur new business. "I have absolutely no doubt that some new clients retained me at least partially to send a message to the leadership that they read the election results and were not ignoring them." Some of those new clients include Bristol-Myers Squibb Co., the Ford Motor Co. and General Mills Inc. VanderJagt said he shared a secretary with two other partners before the Republicans came into power. But now, he has a staff of six working under hi m, including another lawyer and several legislative analysts.

To attract clients, Baker & Hostetler, in conjunction with the Tax Foundation, a Washington think tank, has co-hosted yearly meetings that draw large crowds of lobbyists and some lawmakers to trade information about tax issues. This year's meeting, in late January, included talks by—and opportunities to schmooze with—House Ways and Means Committee chairman Bill Archer, R-Texas, House Minority Leader Richard A. Gephardt, D-Mo., and Kies of the Joint Committee on Taxation, which also is chaired by Archer.

The relationships between the law firm and some of the seminar participants have raised some eyebrows. "I'm troubled by the appearance of having a former partner and his boss, Archer, participating in any kind of program sponsored by a law firm that's clearly designed to develop business," said a prominent Washington tax lawyer who asked not to be named.

But Vander Jagt, a former chairman of the National Republican Congressional Committee, said he is thrilled with the attention that the seminar garnered. "I was honored that so many top-notch people attended," he said. "We had a record 300 people who paid $250 each."

Source: *National Journal*, April 13, 1996, p. 815.

Rollins, Lynn Nofzinger, Kenneth Duberstein, and Lee Atwater (all Reagan White House staff members)—can provide invaluable access for their respective clients that can lead to policy influence. In the words of Ed Rollins:

> I've got many friends who are all through the agencies and equally important, I don't have many enemies ... I tell my clients I can get your case moved to the top of the pile.[2]

This kind of clout is crucial in the game of political influence. The revolving door between governmental personnel and various interests contributes to the formation of issue networks having deep concerns. Such issues include energy policy, child care, health, and education.

Another important Washington lobbying component consists of numerous law firms. A variation exists among them with respect to size, policy concerns, interest group relationships, and governmental contacts. It is not unusual to find former government legal counsels within firm ranks. Jeffrey H. Birnbaum, respected Washington writer, identifies the ten most influential lobbying firms with respect to power and access (see Box 4.3).

In recent years, a number of Washington law firms have expanded their representation. John P. Heinz and his associates found:

> more than one Washington law firmcreates and houses trades associations that are nominally "clients" of the lawyers but are in fact something closer to wholly owned subsidiaries of the law firm ... the law firm typically was instrumental in organizing the trade association ... one of the lawyers serves as executive secretary or director of the association, and the law firm performs management services for the association.[3]

Interest representation, in light of the above, has taken on an entrepreneurial dimension. Given the complexities and risks of various policy processes, highly specialized management and representation are required.

BOX 4.3   Kings of K Street

1. **Verner Liipfert Bernhard McPherson & Hand**   (*Bob Dole, Lloyd Hand, Harry McPherson, John Merrigan, George Mitchell, Ann Richards*)
   Ex-Senators Dole and Mitchell provide the prestige, but wily workhorses like McPherson and Merrigan service New Orleans, Taiwan, Ameritech, and other major clients.
2. **Barbour Griffith & Rogers**   (*Haley Barbour, Lanny Griffith, Ed Rogers*)
   Haley Barbour went straight from chairing the Republican Party to lobbying for huge business interests that range from Big Tobacco to Microsoft to FedEx.
3. **Akin Gump Strauss Hauer & Feld**   (*Joel Jankowsky, Vernon Jordan, Robert Strauss*)
   Heavyweights include Strauss, former head of the Democratic Party, and Vernon Jordan, of Bill-and-Monica fame. But the lobbying genius is ex-Hill aide Jankowsky.
4. **Patton Boggs**   (*Thomas Boggs, John Jonas, Cliff Massa, Donald Moorehead, Stewart Pape*)
   The extremely plugged-in Boggs heads an all-star lobbying roster with 244 clients that run from trial lawyers to Chrysler, and from Bechtel to TRW.

5 Timmons & Co. *(William Cable, Bryce L. Harlow, Timothy Keating, Tom Korologos)*
Korologos, a longtime GOP adviser and lobbyist, runs this small boutique, whose client list includes Dell, the National Rifle Association, and baseball's commissioner.

6 Duberstein Group *(Michael Berman, Steven Champlin, Kenneth Duberstein, Henry Gandy)*
Duberstein graduated from Timmons to head his own small firm with an even more stellar client roster, including General Motors, Goldman Sachs, and United Airlines.

7 O'Brien Calio *(Nicholas Calio, Kim McKerman, Charles Mellody, Lawrence O'Brien III, Linda Tarplin)*
Larry O'Brien III, son of the ex-Kennedy andn Johnson aide, and Nick Calio, President Bush's top lobbyist, represent AT&T, Motorola, Fannie Mae, and Sears.

8 Baker Donelson Bearman & Caldwell *(Howard H. Baker Jr., Keith Kennedy, Jan Powell, James Range, John Tuck)*
Baker, the former Senate Majority Leader and ex-chief of staff for President Reagan, partners with Linda Daschle, wife of the current Senate Minority Leader.

9 Dutko Group *(Gary Andres, Daniel Dutko, Ronald Kaufman, Steve Perry)*
Dutko, a top Democratic fundraiser, and his big-time GOP partners represent a raft of high-tech firms, plus low-tech Union Pacific and the Virgin Islands.

10 Williams & Jensen *(David Franasiak, Robert Glennon, J. Steven Hart, J.D. Williams, David Starr)*
Williams is a renowned fundraiser, tax lobbyist, and duck hunter whose firm has bagged clients like Coca-Cola, Cigna, J.P. Morgan, Texaco, and Genentech.

Source: Jeffrey H. Birnbaum, "Kings of K Street," *Fortune Magazine*, December 7, 1998, p. 137.

LOBBYING STRATEGIES

Before we can draw any meaningful conclusions about lobbyists and their potential for policy influence, we first need to examine their various techniques or strategies of influence. All political organizations want results and they direct their efforts accordingly. It goes without saying that all players use techniques most appropriate to their cause, and these may include one option or several. Furthermore, these techniques of influence may vary over time as the locus of decision making shifts from one area to another.

It must also be kept in mind that organized interests and public officials have different perspectives of each other. For congressional personnel, interest groups represent only one of several forces seeking to influence congressional policymaking. Various appeals from the president, other party leaders, and constituents must also be factored in. For political players, Congress is only one of several institutions with policymaking capabilities. Groups must contend with the president, numerous bureaucratic entities, and the judicial system as well.

DIRECT AND INDIRECT LOBBYING

Generally speaking, lobbying strategies are either direct or indirect. Direct lobbying consists of personal contact between the lobbyist and some targeted public official. Consulting with legislators or their staffs, interacting with agency personnel, or presenting testimony before a law- or rule-making forum are forms of direct lobbying. Indirect lobbying consists of more circuitous methods of influencing policymakers. For example, a group spokesperson may disseminate a video or a newsletter within a congressional district seeking support for or opposition to pending legislation. A media campaign or the establishment of opposition groups with respect to certain actions by the national Food and Drug Administration illustrates other options available to lobbyists for political influence.

Direct lobbying includes a range of options that may not be available to all petitioners. Well-established political interests like the American Farm Bureau Federation, the U.S. Chamber of Commerce, or the American Petroleum Institute are likely to pursue direct lobbying. This is due to their already established relationships with congressional and executive personnel. Additionally, their relatively larger memberships, money, and expertise give them "a leg up" on the smaller and less affluent players like the Gay and Lesbian Task Force, the League of United Latin American Citizens (LULAC), and Population Zero. These latter organizations frequently coalesce with other organizations and mount an indirect or grass-roots lobbying effort to present their claims more effectively.

LOBBYING THE LEGISLATURE

Given Congress's primary role in the drafting and passage of legislation, its members are the focus of continuous and intensive lobbying pressures. Just about every piece of legislation that eventually becomes law involves coalitions of organizations on both sides of the issue. No one legislative experience replicates all the others. Each brings forth its own set of advocates and strategies for or against passage. Box 4.4 on pages 56–57 presents a brief chronology of lobby action against legislation that would update existing clean air standards against legislation that would update existing clean air standards to ban dust particle emissions. Note the plethora of individuals, organizations, and strategies at work in this example.

Legislative lobbying involves providing services as well as making requests. Frequently, interest group spokespersons assist overburdened legislators in a number of important ways such as providing background materials for public statements and speeches, generating data, devising legislative strategies, and serving as liaisons to other lobbies. Provision of these services can establish more positive relationships over time.

Interest spokespersons have also developed a wide range of indirect techniques for pressuring members of Congress. Given the increased legislative turnover in recent years and the weakening of party loyalties, congressional personnel are less tied to tradition. They can be more easily swayed by public opinion polls and petitions by grass-roots organizations. Today, more organizations are availing themselves of modern technology (e.g., computers, overnight mailings, fax machines, etc.) to contact and pressure wavering Congress members. The new technology is available to supplement Washington lobbying as well as to newly formed organizations or coalitions thereof that lack established linkages. Indirect lobbying is not new, but its growing sophistication and magnitude are.

Ideally, the essence of grass-roots pressures lies in generating influence that has the appearance of spontaneity: a "ground swell" of public opinion or widespread expressions of "public concern" over some issue that have legitimacy but do not appear to be orchestrated. Usually, home district pressures do not spring spontaneously from constituencies; this is a political fact of life. Rather, genuine grass-roots pressures are enhanced by actions of public relations firms and group activists feeling strongly about a particular issue (see Box 4.5 on pages 58–63).

One other dimension of indirect lobbying is what can be called electioneering, whereby political players elect their friends and supporters to public office. Interest organizations are inextricably linked to the electoral process. Though initially policy oriented, today's political players appreciate the importance of electoral participation. Labor unions, environmentalists, Christian fundamentalists, veterans, feminists, and so on are participating in a growing number of electoral activities.* This deepening commitment serves two purposes: Group support is a strong inducement for a candidate to support the association's goals, and participation helps ensure that sympathetic officials remain in office.

---

*Emily's List, a feminist organization is dedicated to electing Democratic women to public office. The organization's name is from Early Money Is Like Yeast—it makes the dough (dollars) rise. Early seed money for women candidates allows them to be more successful as candidates and in their fund-raising.

BOX 4.4 Chronology of Lobby Action with Congress

OIL SLICK

How to choke off clean air with independent expenditures. DAVID H. KOCH, 56, Wichita, Kan. Party: R and Libertarian. When the Environmental Protection Agency announced last November it would update Clean Air Act standards to ban dust particle emissions that reportedly cause 40,000 premature deaths annually, big industries sharpened their knives. (Final EPA regulations are due by July.) Oil companies, automakers, and the nations largest manufacturers claim it will cost them billions to comply. Among them is David Koch, chairman of Koch Industries, whose oil subsidiary is being sued by the government for Clean Water Act violations, for a reported $55 million. Although Koch gave $339,000 to federal campaigns in 1995-96, it's only one way he sought influence. He also gives through a tangled web of think tanks, PR agencies, and trade associations, all of which want Congress to gut the Clean Air Act.

HIRED GUN

CITIZENS FOR A SOUND ECONOMY, a lobbying group that advocates "economic freedom," has mobilized a $5 million fake grassroots, or "astroturf" campaign in 10 states to fight the EPA (see "Spin Cycle"). Koch's foundations have given CSE $8 million since 1984.

IN THE TANK

The CATO INSTITUTE's Michael Gough co-wrote an op-ed piece claiming the EPA relied on mere "statistical association." Koch helps fund the libertarian think tank.

CONGRESS

$7,000

In January, Sen. MIKE ENZI (R-Wyo.) compared the EPA proposal to "death by 10,000 slices, and its victim is the American economy." Enzi took $5,000 from KOCHPAC and $2,000 from the Koch family.

$6,000

Sen. JOHN WARNER (R-Va.) sits on a panel that oversees EPA proposals. Weighing in at a February hearing, he said EPA laws are already too strong. He took $5,000 from KOCHPAC and $1,000 from Koch.

BIG TENT

According to the National Association of Manufacturers, Koch Industries is among 700 companies and trade groups that make up the AIR QUALITY STANDARDS COALI-TION, which opposes the EPA's regulations. Run by NAM, the coalition includes Ford, General Motors, and Exxon and reportedly boasts a $2 million war chest.

AQSC's spokesman C. BOYDEN GRAY (#67) was Bush's White House counsel, is chair of Citizens for a Sound Economy, and is a lawyer at the law firm Wilmer, Cutler & Pickering, where his clients include Geneva Steel.

Utah-based GENEVA STEEL has given AQSC $20,000. The EPA cites a 1986 health study linking a Geneva plant's pollution with an increase in local respiratory problems to show the need for tougher laws.

Other AQSC/MoJo 400 members include Detroit Diesel chair/race-car driver ROGER S. PENSKE (#148); William E. Flaherty (#192), whose Horsehead Industries was fined $5.6 million under the Clean Air Act; and Floyd D. Gottwald (#201).

SPIN CYCLE

CSE broadcast ads in Chicago (to coincide with EPA hearings there in January on the new regulations), and in Washington, D.C. One radio spot claimed (falsely) that the proposals would ban fireworks: "Stars and Stripes Forever" played in the background as a narrator said, "Imagine a new government regulation that takes away our freedom to . . . celebrate our freedom."

CONGRESS

$11,500

Rep. DAVID McINTOSH (R-Ind.), chair of a key oversight panel, says the EPA has "overreached." An ex-CSE staffer, he received $8,500 from KOCHPAC; $2,000 from Koch; and $1,000 from Gray.

$6,000

Sen. JAMES INHOFE (R-Okla.) chairs the clean air subcommittee. Echoing Cato, he says the EPA's science relies on "statistical associations." He received $5,000 from KOCHPAC and $1,000 from Gray.

Source: Romesh Ratnesar and John Cook, "Oil Slick," *Mother Jones*, May/June 1997, p. 49.

An increasing range of techniques is being developed and employed by more and more interest groups. These include endorsements, assistance in voter registration, dissemination of campaign literature, get-out-the-vote drives, and of course, financial contributions (covered in the next chapter). Organized labor pioneered the concept of establishing significant support for candidates. The AFL-CIO's Committee on Political Education (COPE) is a modern prototype of the campaign committee. COPE screens candidates for federation support and informs the general membership. These decisions are made on the basis of federation issues rather than the candidates' partisanship. But traditionally, labor has supported Democratic candidates while Republicans have benefited from various corporate supporters.

BOX 4.5   Tobacco Grass-Roots Campaign

BLOWING SMOKE AT ITS CRITICS

Facing myriad regulatory, legal and tax threats from Washington and the states, the tobacco industry has come out smoking. The industry has substantially boosted its Washington and state lobbying operations while heavily tilting its political contributions to the Republicans.

Since the Clinton Administration came into office, the lobbying and political landscape confronting the $45 billion-a-year tobacco industry has changed for the worse in some critical ways. The Food and Drug Administration (FDA)—with the White House's blessings-is getting close to regulating cigarettes as drugs. Separately, the Justice Department is probing whether top industry executives lied under oath in testimony before Congress about nicotine's addictiveness.

Additionally, seven states have filed suit against the tobacco companies in an effort to recover billions in medicaid costs for individuals with smoking-related ailments. Meanwhile, two to three dozen states have been weighing new excise taxes on tobacco products. And dozens of city and local governments have passed new smoking curbs in the past few years.

To fight back, the tobacco industry has poured millions into ever-more-ingenious grass-roots operations and coalition-building efforts. Both tobacco giants, Philip Morris Co. Inc. and RJR Nabisco Holdings Inc., have also given big bucks to think tanks, contributed heavily to political campaigns and retained powerful law firms to boost the beleaguered industry's political fortunes.

Analysts see different forces driving the tobacco industry efforts. "The tobacco industry is fighting legislative and regulatory battles where it's often the Democrats who are its opponents and the Republicans who are its allies," said Josh Goldstein, the research director for the nonpartisan Center for Responsive Politics in Washington, which tracks the influence of money in politics. Tobacco is a regional industry, too, and "the southern states are becoming more and more Republican," he added.

The Winston-Salem (N.C.)-based Ramhurst Corp., established in 1993 with RJR's enthusiastic backing, symbolizes the industry's latest innovations in grass-roots lobbying. Founded by two former RJR grass-roots organizers, Ramhurst taps a loosely knit network of about two dozen part-time political and grass-roots operatives to defend the company's interests. Although it has lined up a few other corporations and trade groups as clients, Ramhurst's chief account is RJR, according to Doug Goodyear, Ramhurst's vice president and treasurer.

And for RJR, opposing FDA regulation of tobacco has been "a big priority," Goodyear said. To generate letters opposing the FDA's regulatory mission, Ramhurst relies on the operatives who run boutique firms in states such as Kansas and Minnesota. Ramhurst's efforts are coordinated with RJR, which maintains sizable files of smokers' rights activists going back to the mid-1980s, when it started organizing such groups nationwide. Michael Phillips, RJR's director of field operations, who oversees Ramhurst's work for the company, said that "we have alerted retailers to the impact that the FDA would have on them."

Still, it has been Ramhurst's outside consultants who have given the fledgling company extra clout with well-connected, mostly Republican politicians who can serve as valuable allies in Washington and in the states. For example, in 1995, House Majority Whip Tom D. Delay, R-Texas, contracted with Ramhurst to hire one of its top consultants, Karl Gallant, to run Delay's leadership political action committee (PAC), Americans for a Republican Majority, according to a story in the May-June issue of *Mother Jones* magazine.

ARMPAC, which was a key tool for Delay in garnering the votes to become whip, has benefited handsomely from its ties to Ramhurst. Last year, ARMPAC, which was heavily involved in Virginia state legislative races, received $73,000 in contributions from RJR out of a total of $175,000 that it raised directly from corporations in unlimited "soft" money. Philip Morris also contributed $10,000 to the Virginia effort. A Delay aide said that similar campaigns are being considered this year in other states-including California, North Carolina and Pennsylvania. ARMPAC will also be hosting at least two dinners and a golf tournament at the GOP convention in San Diego.

Besides running ARMPAC, Gallant has been one of several Ramhurst consultants who have been very active in fighting state excise tax increases on cigarettes. Late last year, for example, Gallant worked in New Jersey alongside antitax groups such as Citizens for a Sound Economy (CSE) to kill an excise tax hike backed by Republican Gov. Christine Todd Whitman.

In 1994-95, Gallant and Ramhurst had a fund-raising contract with Rep. John Shacegg, R-Ariz., a freshman star who became a key ally of the GOP leadership when Speaker Newt Gingrich, R-Ga., tapped him to chair GOPAC, the political action committee that Gingrich ran. Last year Ramhurst also recruited

David Armey, the son of House Majority Leader Richard K. Armey, R-Texas, to be one of its field operatives in Texas and other states. And for additional political and grass-roots muscle, Ramhurst uses Tom Synhorst, a long time political consultant to Senate Majority Leader Robert Dole, R-Kan., who runs Kansas City-based Direct Connect, a telemarketing firm.

Philip Morris, the nation's biggest tobacco company, has also worked hard to cultivate it's grass-roots clout. The National Smokers Alliance (NSA), which the company launched with an estimated $4 million in seed money in late 1993 and which now boasts an estimated three million members nationwide, is also fighting multifront wars for the industry. The NSA, which styles itself a smokers'-rights group, has been pressing its membership through its regular newsletter to write to the agency opposing FDA regulation.

The alliance's clout has been enhanced by a well-connected advisory board that often is asked to help out on key issues. The board includes such prominent figures as former Rep. Guy Vander Jagt, R-Mich., who's now a Washington lobbyist with Baker & Hostetler, the Cleveland law firm; former ABC News correspondent Pierre Salinger, now a Burson-Marsteller consultant; and Jeanie Austin, a former co-chairwoman of the Republican National Committee.

Some board members such as Vander Jagt have written letters to the FDA attacking its regulatory proposals. Vander Jagt, who attended a board meeting in Palm Springs, Fla., in mid-March, said the group has been trying to diversify its corporate support but that Philip Morris is still its leading backer. "Philip Morris is a giant playing in the funding, but less than when it started," he said. "The goal is to be entirely self-sufficient."

The alliance, which has annual dues of $10, has also received some significant support from Brown & Williamson Tobacco Corp., another major cigarette producer, according to sources familiar with the group. Vander Jagt added that at the Florida retreat there was talk of "courting the gaming industry" for support.

To bolster the cause of smokers' rights, the NSA late last year hired the public affairs firm Creative Response Concepts in Alexandria, Va., to help line up talk-radio appearances for William Althaus, the alliance's chairman and former York (Pa.) mayor. In recent months, Althaus has appeared on talk shows in Chicago, Dallas, and New Orleans. The alliance's president, Thomas Humber-a former Burson-Marsteller executive who worked on the Philip Morris account at the firm-has recently expanded the group's PR muscle by luring away an old Burson colleague, Gary Auxier, who also had worked on Philip Morris business, to be its vice president.

The tobacco industry has also bestowed its considerable largess on several influential Washington groups with strong grass-roots capacities. For example, the American Legislative Exchange Council (ALEC), a powerful group of about 3000 conservative state legislators, receives plenty of tobacco money.

Philip Morris gives about $50,000 yearly, RJR approximately $40,000 annually and United States Tobacco Co. (UST) about $15,000 a year to ALEC's coffers, according to an ALEC official.

In an Oct. 4, 1995 newsletter, ALEC urged its members to write to the FDA to voice opposition to proposed regulation. The newsletter approvingly cites the Smokeless Tobacco Council's view that FDA regulation would amount to an "agency power grab" that "flouts Congress's steadfast refusal to give FDA jurisdiction over tobacco."

ALEC has also weighed in with its state affiliates to block efforts in several states to increase excise taxes. On Feb. 23, ALEC's executive director, Daniel B. Denning, wrote to about 20 members of the South Dakota Legislature, which was weighing an excise tax hike, and reminded them that ALEC has long warned of the "negative effect of such taxes on economic growth."

Another prominent ally in the fight against excise taxes on cigarettes is CSE, a conservative Washington think tank and grass-roots Goliath that has worked closely with the GOP leadership on many issues. Besides its campaign in New Jersey last year, CSE was a leader in a 1992 effort against a proposed increase in the New York excise tax. According to two former CSE members, the group received about $250,000 a year in the early 1990s from Philip Morris to help launch its state affiliates in New Jersey, New York, and four other states.

On another state front, the tobacco industry has turned to its premier Washington law firm of Covington & Burling to lead the fight to dissuade state attorneys general from filing suits against the industry. Covington partner Keith Teel visited several state attorneys general in what appears to be a largely successful lobbying effort to block the suits from being filed. Louisiana, Massachusetts and Texas-three states that Teel visited, have filed suits. Teel has been accompanied on his rounds by former Virginia Attorney General Andrew P. Miller, a partner at the Washington law firm of Dickstein, Shapiro, & Morin.

In the past year or two, tobacco largesse has also gone increasingly to help state officials who the industry thinks could be useful allies in its drive to block excise taxes and litigation. RJR and Philip Morris each chip in about $40,000 a year to the Republican Governors Association's elite governors' board, which is made up of approximately 16 corporate sponsors. And on Feb. 5, Philip Morris chairman Geoffrey C. Bible chaired an association dinner in Washington. The tobacco company underwrote the event with a $100,000 contribution. Seizing the moment, Bible delivered a wide-ranging talk about how the tobacco industry creates jobs at home and boosts exports abroad.

Just 11 days after the dinner, Gov. Kirk Fordice, R-Miss., filed an unusual suit against Mississippi Attorney General Michael Moore, who in mid-1994 had been the first state attorney general in the country to bring litigation against the industry to recoup medicaid costs. Fordice's suit asserted that Moore had exceeded his authority by suing the tobacco industry.

Meanwhile, tobacco contributions have undergone seismic shifts to the Republicans that coincide with the Clinton Administration's attacks on the industry and the GOP's capture of congress. Last year, the two leading soft money donors to the GOP campaign committees were Philip Morris and RJR. Philip Morris gave $975,149 in soft money, and RJR contributed $696,450 to the GOP party committees. In marked contrast, Philip Morris gave $199,000 and RJR $126,250 to the Democrats in 1993-94.

In 1995, tobacco PACs favored GOP Members of Congress by almost 3-1 over Democrats. Republican members received $841,120; Democrats, only $281,000. In 1993, when the Democrats controlled Congress, they had a thin edge, $477,022 to $422,221.

Some Republicans think there are risks for the GOP in such close affiliations with special interests such as the tobacco lobby. "People believed we were going to be different," said Rep. Linda A. Smith, R-Wash., a sponsor of campaign finance reform legislation that would ban PAC contributions. "I think the party has to look at its image. Every decision we make could be perceived as being affected by money unless we change the system."

Still, there's little doubt that the tobacco industry has been sitting pretty in Congress since the Republicans gained power in the 1994 elections. Early on, one of its major congressional champions, House Commerce Committee chairman Thomas J. Bliley Jr. of Virginia, whose district is home to a major Philip Morris plant, made it clear that tobacco would not face new regulations on his watch.

But the industry has also worked hard to develop support among the GOP leadership. Three of the four top House leaders—DeLay, Armey, and House Republican Conference chairman John Boehner of Ohio—signed a letter last December opposing the FDA's proposed regulation of tobacco. So did Dole. The letter was also signed by some prominent Democrats, including Senate Minority Leader Thomas A. Daschle of South Dakota and Sen. Sam Nunn of Georgia.

Looking ahead to this fall's elections, the tobacco industry appears to be banking heavily on the presidential candidacy of Dole. Historically, the tobacco industry has been very generous to Dole and he has been one of its staunchest allies.

Consider the Better America Foundation, a tax-exempt group that Dole set up in 1993 as a Republican think tank. Of the $4.5 million that the group raised before Dole pulled the plug on the foundation last June, about 5 percent came from the tobacco industry. RJR and Philip Morris each donated $100,000 to the foundation, and U.S. Tobacco kicked in $50,000.

Tobacco interests have also lavished their riches on the Dole Foundation, a charity for the disabled that is linked to the Senator. In 1994, the foundation received donations from Philip Morris, RJR, the Tobacco Institute, the Smokeless Tobacco Council and the Flue Cured Tobacco Cooperative-Stabilization Corp.

Part of the foundation's success is attributable to Edward Kratovil, a UST executive who's on the Dole Foundation board and raises money for it. Indeed, UST has long treated Dole royally. Dole, who often flies on corporate planes for his campaign appearances, has used the UST corporate jet about two dozen times and is frequently accompanied by Kratovil, according to industry sources. What's more, UST was a leading backer of Campaign America, Dole's former leadership PAC, chipping in $32,000 in 1993-94 alone, according to the Center for Responsive Politics.

The ties between the company and Dole go way back. In 1986, Dole earned the industry's fealty when several Members of Congress were pushing for hefty increases on smokeless tobacco products. Dole rode to the rescue by sponsoring an amendment that set a tax on smokeless products at about one-eighth the rate for cigarettes. A public health advocate has estimated that since its passage, the Dole amendment has saved UST about $250 million.

To Michael Pertschuk, a co-director of the Advocacy Institute, a non-profit group that has pushed for tougher curbs on smoking, the industry's contributions have historical roots. "The tobacco companies recognize that they're in very deep trouble," he said. "They're investing more in what has paid off for them in the past. They've found willing takers in the new Republicans as well as some of the old Democrats."

Source: National Journal, April 20, 1996, pp. 884-887.

LOBBYING THE EXECUTIVE

Given the dramatic size and growth of the executive branch over the past quarter century, it is not surprising that it is an increasing target for group penetration. By tradition, most lobbyists have been far less interested in bureaucratic policymaking than in legislative policymaking. But because the Congress has seen fit to add to the size and responsibilities of various bureaucratic units, executive lobbying has grown proportionally. Additionally, bureaucratic profiles vary from one agency to another as Table 4.1 on page 64 demonstrates. Ideology and party affiliation are relatively more important indicators of political compatibility than social background. In the Congress, when Democrats are in control, staffers are much more likely to be Democratic and liberal, and when Republicans are in control, staff personnel are Republican and more conservative. In the bureaucracy, the policy-sensitive positions are monopolized by those who are both partisan and in ideological sympathy with the president. In lower level positions, partisanship and ideology tend to be more pluralistic.

TABLE 4.1   **Personal Background Characteristics of Officials by Government Branch and Policy Domain (Percentages)**

	GOVERNMENT BRANCH			DOMAIN		
	Legislative	*Executive*	*Agriculture*	*Energy*	*Health*	*Labor*
Women	12	7	12	5	18	4
Jewish	9	15	7	10	14	16
Catholic	24	13	10	18	22	26
Type I Protestant	14	27	17	18	22	26
Northeast origin	30	34	23	29	40	37
Southern/ Western origin	37	42	47	49	28	34
Law degree	45	23	23	39	17	55
Other advanced degree	27	50	44	33	54	23
N(=300)	150	150	73	80	73	74

Note: Percentage is of the officials who possess the designated characteristic, within each branch or domain.
    (Source: Reprinted by permission of the publisher from *The Hollow Core* by John P. Heinz, Edward O. Laumann, Robert L. Nelson, and Robert H. Salisbury, Cambridge, Mass: Harvard University Press, Copyright ©1993 by the President and Fellows of Harvard College).

Agency mission also conditions lobbying strategies. For example, health policies are impacted by funding levels. Health and Human Services personnel are quite sensitive to the spiraling costs of Medicare and Medicaid along with those of medical research. On the other hand, labor policies turn on issues of public regulation and statutory authority. Lobbying approaches, then, turn on the number of personnel as well as organizational factors.

Speaking of the latter, at what level—cabinet secretary, undersecretary, assistant secretary, middle management—is pressure best applied? More often than not, efforts are concentrated at the top of the authority structure, where greater power over policy probably exists. It must be kept in mind that policy dominance does not fit a neat hierarchical arrangement but is broad and diffuse. Patterns of interaction may reflect the levels of conflicts surrounding a certain policy issue such as national health insurance. In comparison, interaction over labor policy will be quite low.

Lobbying intensity varies across the executive establishment. The National Labor Relations Board (NLRB) is not as heavily lobbied as the Pentagon or Health and Human Services. National bureaucrats, though diverse, do have relatively distinct backgrounds and responsibilities. Once in office, they serve as liaisons both to Congress and the interest group community. They constitute a distinct political cadre that serves as gatekeepers to national policymaking.

A very recent development that may very well revolutionize some aspects of today's lobbying activities can be categorized as "cyber-lobbying." The use cable satellite television, which allows for instantaneous communication between constituents and various public officials, is at hand. As Box 4.6 shows, the Internet is becoming a grass-roots tool for outreach as well as keeping constituents informed. A cyber-polity has come into being that includes millions of voters and an endless number of lobbyists, journalists, officeholders, researchers, and congressional staffers.

Box 4.6 Mr. Smith E-Mails Washington: Constituents On Line

At 1:15 p.m. on a recent Tuesday afternoon, exactly 316 computers are logged onto C-SPAN's World Wide Web site on the internet.

Tom Patton, C-SPAN's new-media manager, watches the connections light up on his computer screen like fireflies on a summer night. He reads off where the 316 are from: Texas, Virginia, Georgia, California, Florida, Oregon. The list of places goes on and on, punctuated at long last by Japan and Pakistan.

"We get use from all over the planet," Patton said. The internet "cuts across everything."

The explosion of Internet resources flowing from Capitol Hill is creating a small but rapidly growing cyber-polity who use them. The consumer revolution in the Internet is making cyberspace less the domain of academics and computer wonks and more the terrain of average Americans. And as Internet technology becomes even more common and accessible, the potential constituents of the electronic Congress will look even more like middle-America.

"It's not just young white male geeks with thick glasses and calculators in their shirt pockets anymore," Patton said. Indeed, all types of people, young and old, are hanging out on the Internet these days.

The cyber-polity is growing to include the typical cast of Capitol Hill characters such as lobbyists, journalists, researchers and congressional staff.

But more and more, it's a diverse crowd of concerned citizens and distant Congress-watchers who are becoming cyber-constituents, firing up their Web browsers and talking politics through their modems.

By and large, they're a politically savvy bunch with more than a few C-SPAN regulars in their ranks. Though some are techies with their own Web pages, not all are technical wizards. All they need to know is how to point and click a computer mouse to where they want to go. And they have a kind of access to Congress that their off-line peers don't.

The cyber-constituents enjoy their instant, first-hand access to congressional documents. They enjoy firing off e-mail to their representatives in Congress. And they like feeling closer to Congress, whether they are politics junkies or just want to keep a watchful eye on their elected officials.

"If some member has done what I consider a bang-up job on some piece of legislation, special orders or hearing, I drop him or her an e-mail expressing my feeling," said Dorothy Clapp, a 55-year old legal assistant from California and a self-described politics fanatic.

The growth of the Internet political community is staggering. Just last year, roughly 35 million people were using the Internet. By this year, that number had boomed to 55 million, a 57 percent increase. In 1996, consumers for the first time bought more computers than they did televisions.

That growth is reflected in traffic on congressional Internet sites. For example, the number of times the House of Representatives' home page (www.house.gov) is accessed grew from 2.7 million in January to 9.5 million in October. While these connections, or "hits," can be misleading-they count each time someone accesses or returns to a page, not how often they visit an entire site-no one doubts that the use of congressional web sites is skyrocketing.

But with many Internet watchers making wide-eyed predictions about technology changing the nature of elections and governing, determining the cyber-constituency is a task that will be embraced by lawmakers and candidates for Congress.

"By the congressional off-year elections in 1998, the presence of ordinary voters in political web sites should be obvious," wrote Wayne Rash, Jr., author of a book called *Politics on the Net: Wiring the Political Process.*

"By 2000, it will be too great to ignore," Rash wrote.

Researchers with the Government and Politics on the Net Project at the University of California, Santa Barbara, are searching for an answer with a pair of survey snapshots.

A nationwide phone survey was aimed at pinning down the potential cyber-constituency: all adults, politics fans or not, who both have Internet access and actually use it on a daily basis. The survey found a potential constituency of a little under 10 percent of all adults (roughly 20 million). They have a median age of about 37, and are predominantly male (65 percent). Not surprisingly for avid computer users, they are educated (60 percent had college degrees) and have money (their median income is $57,000).

A second survey is narrowing the view to those who actually use political and government-oriented web sites. It found that users of these types of sites are faithful voters, are politically active and are about evenly split among Democrats, Republicans and independents.

Participants took the survey from several non-partisan public affairs sites such as the Library of Congress' THOMAS and the U.S. League of Women Voters' site. Though the analysis is incomplete and comes from a non-random sample, early results are still telling: 95 percent said they were registered to vote, while 29 percent said they had donated money to political candidates. Eighteen percent—well above average—said they had volunteered for political campaigns.

Likewise, they're not easily swayed. The cyber-constituents are more likely to be strong partisans than the general public.

The initial results seem to show that, at least for now, the cyber-constituents are mostly the same people who were already involved in politics and government in the first place. If they didn't have the Web, they would still learn about Congress from television, radio or newspapers. If they didn't have e-mail, they would still send letters, faxes and make calls to the Capitol.

The evidence, said University of California researcher Bruce Bimber, suggests that claims that the Internet is changing democratic government aren't panning out just yet. "Rather than doing what some had hoped—to draw back into public life the alienated, those who don't vote or mistrust the government—the Internet seems to be just another instrument in the tool kit of the politically engaged."

Some disagree with this assessment. Measured by the e-mail responses some Hill offices are getting, technology has made contacting a member of Congress easier than ever. It has something to do with the speed and ease of sending e-mail, as opposed to sitting down to pen a letter. And e-mail, unlike U.S. mail, doesn't cost 32 cents a pop.

"There's a whole group that's emerged that wouldn't be politically active in any way if they didn't have a computer," said Wayne D'Angelo, system administrator for Bob Franks, R-N.J. "They've grown politically active through e-mail. We've never gotten a letter from them."

Keeping Tabs on Congress

While the Internet's impact on representative democracy remains an open question, it clearly has been a force for those with their palm on a mousepad.

C-SPAN's Patton said that when the cable network broadcast the Senate's campaign finance hearings over the Web, he got e-mail from viewers who said they had bought computers for the occasion.

That was the only way people outside the hearing room could watch. Both C-SPAN television channels were showing House and Senate floor proceedings.

For those who are using it, the Internet can be a powerful tool that brings Congress closer. Some see the mountains of raw information available, from bill texts to committee testimony to the Congressional Record, as the key to closer scrutiny of elected officials.

Clapp, for example, said she downloaded the text of the abortion bill President Clinton vetoed last month, and incorporated it into a stinging letter she sent to the White House.

"Now I can find the raw information, instead of having to rely on that filtered through the media or interpreted for me by a politician," Clapp said.

Chip Freundt, a 40-year old Mississippian with diabetes, also keeps tabs on Congress over the Internet. He uses the Web to track legislation related to diabetes and disability generally, and frequently zips off e-mail to Republican Sen. Thad Cochran of Mississippi and other members.

Likewise, the Internet is finding a place in the political community as a grass-roots organizing tool. One strength e-mail has over regular mail or the telephone is that informing or mobilizing masses of people is as easy as pressing the "send" key.

One way such e-mail finds its way to the Hill—often to the annoyance of staff members—is as "spam" messages, those sent to dozens or even hundreds of members' offices in a single shot.

But the Internet is becoming an essential grass-roots tool for outreach and for keeping the interested informed.

Jesse Cooday, a Native American of the Tlingit Nation, said the Internet is injecting new life into his peoples' long-time cause—reclaiming some of their native southeast Alaska lands.

"In 1995, Haa tl'atgi—the first Landless Tlingit Internet Support Group—was formed to bring our story to the Internet community," said Cooday, who also uses the name Shoowee Ka'.

One page on the site directs other on-line Tlingits and their supporters outside Alaska to the House's "Write your Representative" e-mail site, and includes the names, addresses, fax and phone numbers of key congressional players on Native American issues.

The page also helps the Tlingits, some 4,000 miles from Washington, to take the pulse of congressional debate on Native American issues. A good example is the Senate debate last September on a section of the fiscal 1998 Interior appropriations bill.

"On C-SPAN, I watched the Senate floor debate on the American Indian Sovereignty issue," Cooday said. "Then later, I went into the Senate Committee on Indian Affairs' Web site, copied the complete floor debate, and posted it to our Web page. Within hours, other natives back home with computers made copies and passed them around to others without access to cable TV or the Internet. Everyone back home knows that a lot is riding on this issue."

Source: Congressional Quarterly, Weekly Report," Fall 1998, pp. 47–48.

Lobbyists and lobbying have become an indispensable part of our political processes. Once scorned as a corruptive influence, the lobbying profession serves to link government and citizen organizations in common pursuits. To be sure, a good deal of lobbying is done on behalf of well-organized interests, often to the detriment of the unorganized. But as discussed here, current policymaking virtually requires the technical expertise and knowledge that lobbyists can provide. Governmental decision making at all levels incorporates both the political and substantive information of various lobbying interests.

NOTES

1. Quoted in John L. Zorack, *The Lobbying Handbook: A Comprehensive Lobbying Guide* (Washington, DC: Professional Lobbying and Consulting Center, 1990), p. 721.
2. Quoted in *National Journal,* 18, May 3, 1986, p. 1052.
3. See John P. Heinz, Edward O. Laumann, Robert L. Nelson, and Robert H. Salisbury, *The Hollow Core: Private Interests in National Policy Making* (Cambridge, MA: Harvard University Press, 1993), p. 382.

5

The Money Game

Political Action Committees and Soft Money

INTRODUCTION

Political action committees (PACs) are increasingly visible and active forces in today's electoral politics. Some PACs (affiliated) have sponsors such as a labor union, a professional organization, or a corporation. Other PACs (unaffiliated) are largely autonomous and directed by single or relatively few individuals such as taxpayers, political conservatives, women, and so on. Ostensibly, both types raise and spend money on behalf of selected candidates.

Soft money can involve campaign funds that are solicited and spent by state and local parties for various activities. For purposes of discussion, PACs and their growing political role in American elections are discussed first and then an analysis of soft money donations in the 1996 election is presented. The chapter concludes with a discussion of the efficacy of reforming current campaign finance laws.

POLITICAL ACTION COMMITTEES

As PACs have multiplied and gained increasing public visibility because of their political donations, they have become a primary source of citizen cynicism and growing distrust of national politics in general. Many current writers, journalists, and even politicians demonstrate growing unease with respect to the number of PACs and the money they spend to influence electoral results.[1] However, before a subjective judgment can be made, a more thorough analysis of the PAC phenomenon is in order. Thus, political action committees are discussed chronologically from the standpoint of certain motivational factors in their establishment and challenges to the major parties, with some analysis of their growing financial contributions. In this broader context, a relatively better understanding of PACs in the political process can be gained.

A Brief History

Well into the twentieth century, neither corporations nor labor unions contributed to political campaigns in a significant manner. Corporations, incidentally, were kept from doing so by law, although unions were not. Beginning in the 1930s, unions began contributing to ensure Franklin Roosevelt's reelection as well as the election of prolabor members to Congress in 1936. Growing concern over labor's increasing political contributions led to congressional enactment of the Smith–Connally Act in the early 1940s. Though its primary purpose was to prohibit labor strikes for the duration of World War II, it also banned union political contributions for the duration of the war.

But the passage of Smith–Connally did not deter organized labor's determination to remain involved in the electoral process. In 1943, the Congress of Industrial Organization (CIO) established CIO-PAC. Although unions per se could not make direct contributions from their treasuries under Smith–Connally, the act did not prevent union contributions through its PAC. The CIO was not a union, technically speaking, but it established a "dollar drive" through its membership, and the solicited funds were channeled to candidates through CIO-PAC. In the 1944 elections, this new organization contributed approximately $2 million to candidates.[2]

In 1947, a Republican Congress passed the Taft–Hartley Act, which banned contributions and lobbying expenditures from both labor unions and corporations. Despite these restrictions, labor and business continued to raise and spend money on behalf of selected candidates. Although these activities were challenged in court, the Supreme Court did not rule directly on the constitutionally of these contributions. Both business and labor interpreted this reluctance on the part of the court to mean that as long as political contributions did not come directly out of their respective treasuries they would be tolerated.

Wanting a firmer legal basis for its campaign contributions, organized labor pushed for authorizing legislation in the early 1970s. Its vehicle was the Federal Election Campaign Act (FECA, 1971). This bill had its own political inertia because of the rising costs of campaigning caused by the introduction of television into the electoral process. A Federal Communications

Commission report stated that between 1965 and 1970 candidate spending on television had doubled to $60 million and had tripled since 1962.[3] As a result, the 1971 act established limits on expenditures for communications media by candidates, ceilings (or amounts candidates could contribute to their own campaigns), and a reporting system for both contributions and expenditures.

During congressional consideration of FECA, a key amendment was offered at the request of organized labor.* It was to allow "the establishment, administration, and solicitation of funds to a separate, segregated fund to be utilized for political purposes." This fund was not to contain membership dues or any other monies as a condition of employment or obtained through any commercial transaction. Labor's clear intent was to legitimize its political contribution. This amendment was accepted and became part of the 1971 law.** In 1971, the law and the Supreme Court's decision in *Pipefitters* opened the floodgates for the explosion of PACs in the years immediately following. Initially, labor PACs outnumbered business PACs, but business PACs soon quickly outpaced those of labor (see Table 5.1 on page 76).

Another important element PAC history is the Watergate scandal. This involved a break-in at the Watergate Hotel, location of the Democratic party headquarters in 1972. The perpetrators were caught. A select committee of the Senate investigating the break-in uncovered numerous violations of existing campaign finances such as money "laundering," compiling an "enemies list," and extorting large sums of money from companies like Gulf Oil, American Airlines, and Braniff Airways. Millions of dollars were compiled in a secret fund under the direct control of the Nixon White House. With rising public demands that these practices be outlawed, Congress passed FECA (1974). The provisions of this act included:

contribution limits for individuals, parties, and political action committees;

establishment of the Federal Election Commission (FEC) to administer the law, issue regulations, and receive reports;

setting expenditure limits for parties and presidential candidates accepting public funding; and

establishment of requirements for reporting (disclosing) sources and amounts of campaign contributions and expenditures.

---

*The amendment was offered by Orville Hansen, Republican from Idaho.
**At approximately the same time that Congress was considering FECA (1971), the Supreme Court in *Pipefitters Local Union #562* v. *United States* upheld the right of labor unions to make political contributions as long as (a) the contributions came from political funds that were voluntary and (b) the funds were strictly segregated from any funds emanating from union dues.

FECA (1971) provided for the public funding of presidential campaigns through a $1 checkoff on federal income tax returns. Presidential candidates accepting public funding cannot accept PAC funds during the campaign.

In 1976, the Supreme Court in *Buckley* v. *Valeo*[4] ruled that 1974 FECA limits on candidates' contributions to their own campaigns, limits on campaign expenditures by candidates, and limits on independent committee expenditures were all restrictions of the First Amendment right of free speech and, therefore, unconstitutional. The decision, however, did uphold the law's aggregate expenditure limits for presidential candidates accepting public funding. It also left in place the FEC's limits on contributions from individuals and groups to federal candidates, political committees, and political parties.

The Court's ruling on independent expenditures—contributions independent of candidates' committees, without collusion, consultation, or cooperation—opened the way for widespread independent spending by PACs created by individuals and small groups.

The situation now is quite ironic. Reformers of the early 1970s originally intended to regulate campaign contributions, control spiraling campaign costs, and eliminate undue influences of special interests by encouraging more individual donors. Yet, the reverse has occurred. There are several thousand PACs today spending even more money on behalf of certain candidates. Political action committees are the "bastard children" of FECA legislation: They were not planned for, and their consequences have been totally unanticipated. Frank Sorauf concludes:

> So, the single issue or single configuration of issues is replacing in part the broad, all-encompassing political parties, and the new activism is more selective and less partisan. Combined with the decline of the parties' role in campaigns, this new style of politics increasingly produces candidates who ... organize their own campaigns, assembling the resources and directing their spending. All in all, the new campaign politics fits the PACs like the proverbial glove.[5]

PAC FORMATION: MOTIVATIONAL FORCES

Approximately 4000 PACs that vary both in size and structure exist today. Figure 5.1 gives a breakdown with respect to the general types of PACs in existence through 1996. Table 5.1 on page 76 shows the number of PACs that were in existence at the start of the last ten election cycles. PACs categorized as "other" are sponsored by cooperatives and nonstock corporations.

The greatest number of PACs is generally aligned with business interests. More than 40 percent of all PACs today are associated with corpora-

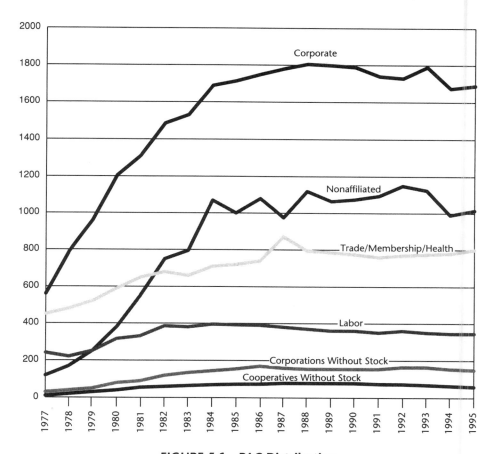

FIGURE 5.1   PAC Distribution

tions (see Table 5.1). Examples are Business-Industry PAC (BIPAC), the Ford Motor Company Civic Action Fund, Sun Oil Company Political Action Committee (SunPAC), and Coca Cola PAC. The next largest group is nonaffiliated PACs such as Americans for Democratic Action (ACE), People for the American Way (PAW), and the American Conservative Union (ACU). Labor unions were once a major source of campaign contributions, but now they rank third. These include such organizations as the Airline Pilots Association International, American Federation of Teachers, Communications Workers of America, and the International Ladies Garment Workers Union. All of the foregoing unions are affiliated with the AFL-CIO.

It must be kept in mind that the PAC universe is quite small compared to the whole political system. PACs are not the ubiquitous tools of organized interests. Indeed, they are dwarfed by the major political parties and

TABLE 5.1 PACs by Election Cycle

	Corporate	Labor	Trade	Nonaffiliated	Other	Total
Jan. 1, 1999	1547	321	821	915	154	3798
Jan. 1, 1997	1642	332	838	1103	164	4079
Jan. 1, 1995	1660	333	792	980	189	3954
Jan. 1, 1993	1735	347	770	1145	198	4195
Jan. 1, 1991	1795	346	774	1062	195	4172
Jan. 1, 1989	1816	354	786	1116	197	4269
Jan. 1, 1987	1744	384	745	1077	207	4157
Jan. 1, 1985	1682	394	698	1053	182	4009
Jan. 1, 1983	1469	380	649	723	150	3371
Jan. 1, 1981	1206	297	576	374	98	2551
Jan. 1, 1979	785	217	453	162	36	1653

Source: Telephone contact to the Federal Election Commission by the author.

other political players concerned with national policy making. In addition, some gaps exist. Washington-based interests organized around occupations in the nonprofit sector are excluded.

FACTORS CONTRIBUTING TO PAC FORMATION

What factors help determine whether or not organized interests establish a PAC? First is the nature of the group's political environment.[6] Where stakes are high and competition is intense, conditions are conducive for PAC formation. These conditions include the opposition and/or division between the major parties over issues important to the player or group.

Second is the intensity and complexity of the organization's lobbying activities. If lobbying activities cover a broad front (e.g., several committees and subcommittees), a range of contacts must be established and maintained. This requires increased expenditures of resources.

Third is the group's emphasis on representation and policy advocacy. For some interests, these are not important functions. Certain professional societies and trade associations utilize various conferences and published works to keep members informed. Other players, though, maintain large Washington establishments because they are convinced that PACs are essential to advocate the policy positions of members and to represent these positions before public agencies and congressional committees.

PACs are more likely to emerge, then, where interest groups face a stable, partisan structure of conflict with respect to policy influence and where they successfully represent their members' interest before relevant public officials.

PACs AND POLICY ORIENTATION

As already shown, different types of interests take contrasting stands across a broad array of issues. As a result, PAC patterns show a distinctive bias in the policy views of their sponsors. Generally speaking, a major aspect of this bias is the weak representation of liberal standpoints among today's PACs.

Organized interests are likely to establish a PAC when there are political incentives for doing so and because their revenues fit existing campaign finance laws. Though interest orientation with respect to such issues as transportation, education, management of the economy, or foreign affairs is important in PAC formation, institutional considerations may outweigh it. Evidence shows that interests in certain policy domains high in PAC formation tend not to get revenues from government such as grants, gifts from firms or individuals, support from religious institutions, or money from private foundations. On the other hand, groups of moderate or low PAC formation (see Table 5.1) may receive financial donations from such sources. They are also more likely to represent a coalition of members' views and opinions rather than advocating policy or some cause. As one source notes:

> PACs flourish only where they can draw on the resources of social or economic institutions; that capability is particularly strong only for businesses connected to narrow segments of the profit sector, such as single corporations or industries; and groups in the nonprofit sector generally cannot apply their institutional resources to electoral activities.[7]

In sum, then, institutional and organizational factors exert greater influence over PAC formation than does a high rate of political conflict over such issues as government regulation of economy, civil rights, or education.

Finally, returning to an earlier point, the PAC system represents a narrower and more conservative universe than the overall interest group system. PACs are generally more interested in economic policies than social policies like education, civil rights, and civil liberties. As noted in this discussion, the PAC system disproportionately represents occupational, profit-driven interests and underrepresents interests of citizen-oriented organizations.

PACs AND POLITICAL PARTIES

The levels of cooperation between political parties and organized interests reflect longstanding relationships based on policy preference, ideological affinities, and shared constituencies. These relationships between groups and the party in government provide an important context for understanding how the various organizations and their PACs relate to the party system: how to access governmental decision makers, how to establish and maintain an effective PAC, and the degree of partisanship that must be factored in when distributing campaign contributions.

If interest groups utilize campaign contributions to enhance their access to sympathetic legislators, PAC contributions then will follow. Thus, conservative interests contribute to Republican candidates and officeholders, and liberal PACs do the same for Democrats. Certainly, a degree of partisanship is present here. There are data, however, showing that business PACs are bipartisan, even though most of the money goes to Republicans. Citizen-oriented and labor PACs are more partisan, giving a higher percentage of their donations to Democrats. Further, a relationship between PACs and parties exists with respect to the level of cooperation donors receive. During the Reagan administrations, for example, conservative PACs and others favoring a less intrusive federal government contributed heavily to Republican candidates for office. This period also saw a sharp increase in conservative PACs. In contrast, those opposed to Reagan's defunding of various public programs contributed heavily through PACs to Democratic candidates. At this same time, there was a corresponding spurt in the formation of liberal PACs. As one source notes:

> [T]he kinds of interest groups aligned with Democratic administrations had a very narrow occupational or institutional bade on which to build, so they reacted to the aggressive conservatism of President Reagan's first term by mobilizing more resources *within* a more or less fixed institutional base and by expanding the number of mostly nonconnected citizen PACs, that is, PACs *without* direct occupational or institutional ties.[8]

Additionally, other liberal citizen associations that had the potential of serving as a fertile organizing ground for additional pro-Democratic PACs did not formalize. Most had no parent organization to help absorb organizing and administrative costs, so they tended to be marginal, ineffective players.

While many have held that the rise of PACs means the demise of parties, evidence here does not support this view. PACs have not emerged from special "subgovernments" that seek to set policy in isolation. Rather, they have emerged from forces that are sensitive to partisan conflict and electoral change. Campaign contributions in this context are a means of overcoming political complexity and volatility, not a way of displacing parties. While it is true that many PACs favor one party over the other, their contributions are usually rationally based on who their supporters are. The rise and political activism of PACs have catalyzed both major parties. Both are much more dedicated to raising their own funds for candidates and pushing for more rebuilding at the grass roots. These additional funds also make more high-tech assistance available to the national parties (e.g., videos, mass mailings, polling, etc.). In a way, then, the base of parties appears to have broadened, not eroded, as a result of PAC formation and resultant activities.

INTERNAL OPERATIONS OF PACs

Today's political action committees display a variety of structures and internal operations. To appreciate how affiliated or nonaffiliated PACs allocate money, we need a general overview of these internal processes and structures.

The affiliated PAC, of course, is subject to the political preferences of its sponsor. A corporate sponsor, for example, pays for the PAC's operations, monitors the PAC's allocative decisions, and provides overall guidance and direction to campaign spending. In practice, this involves the establishment of a PAC governing board drawn from the corporate hierarchy. The board usually reflects the corporation's operational unit (e.g., a plant, a department, or some subsidiary). Labor unions and associational PACs are headed by locally elected officials, who may meet periodically with member representatives. The AFL-CIO's Committee on Political Education works with various state and local unions with respect to the disbursement of campaign funds.

PAC boards are relatively autonomous. They depend a good deal on a permanent staff that is responsible for day-to-day operations while compiling and evaluating candidate information, state electoral data, and federal regulations pertaining to PAC operations.

Nonaffiliated or independent PACs are governed quite differently. No board or other organizational governance exists. Usually, a single individual or a small coterie of insiders calls the shots with no peer review. Many independent PACs are founded and maintained by a single entrepreneur such as Paul Brown's Life Amendment Political Action Committee (LAPAC), Paul Weyrich's Committee for the Survival of a Free Congress (CSFC), or the late Terry Dolan's National Conservative Political Action Committee (NCPAC). Political writer Frank Sorauf characterizes these latter types as "extensions of the ego or persona of one individual."[9] The political goals and objectives of these PACs reflect the homogeneous policy and/or ideological preferences of their founders and leaders.

ALLOCATION DECISIONS

Deciding which candidates to support—and how much to contribute—is, of course, a subjective judgment within each PAC. Most PACs develop their own criteria in this regard. This does not preclude, however, utilizing information gained from other PACs, from national political party officials, and from governmental reports. In spite of unique concerns, a generalized list of PAC criteria would include:

Incumbents

1. What is the candidate's voting record on issues that concern the organization?
2. What are the candidate's committee and subcommittee assignments?
3. What are the characteristics of the candidate's electoral district? Does it have business facilities? Labor unions? Is it urban, suburban, rural? What is the prevailing level of partisanship?

4. What is the candidate's orientation with respect to the organization and its goals?
5. How much money does the candidate need?

Challengers

1. Who is the campaign manager? How experienced and how effective is this person?
2. What is the campaign budget and how much has been raised?
3. Who is doing the campaign polling and what are the latest results?
4. Does the challenger have a reasonable chance of defeating the incumbent?
5. What is the candidate's first choice of committee assignments (must be compatible with the organization's legislative goals)?
6. What are the candidate's views on at least three issues important to the organization?

Ideologically oriented political interests (liberal vs. conservative) publish periodic "report cards" or "issue ratings" on members of Congress. Players like the Right-to-Life Committee PAC, the National Christian Action Coalition, and the Committee for the Survival of a Free Congress regularly use "passing" or "failing" grades to rate members of Congress with respect to campaign donations.

A candidate with a passing grade on a series of votes has the opportunity to receive funding from the evaluation player. Challengers, not having a voting record, receive questionnaires addressing issues of concern to a PAC's sponsoring organization. Or challengers may be quizzed at a party function or a convention with respect to such issues as abortion, food stamps, collective bargaining, or tuition tax credit for parents of college students.

Although most PACs promote the financial fortunes of selected candidates, some unaffiliated PACs indulge in what can be called "negative spending," that is, defeating certain political enemies. During the 1980s, for example, the National Conservative Political Action Committee spent heavily to defeat liberal candidates.* Its former head, Terry Dolan, asserted, "A group like ours can lie through its teeth, and the candidate stays clean."[10] Thus, various distortions of the candidate's voting record or persona are strategies to be utilized.

---

*NCPAC targets of negative spending in the recent past are Senators Edward Kennedy, Paul Sarbanes, and former Senator Lowell Weicker. NCPAC targets in the House were Dan Rostenkowski, former Speaker Jim Wright, and Robert Edger.

SOFT MONEY AND POLITICAL CAMPAIGNS

An increasingly important dimension of player involvement in campaign finance involves "soft money" (contributions by national parties to state parties to encourage greater voter participation through voter registration, party building, and get-out-the-vote drives). The 1996 elections are a high-water mark in the amount of soft money raised and spent by both major parties. Some $263.5 million in soft money was raised and spent in 1995–1996 to influence various electoral outcomes across the nation.[11] This money has come to be recognized as the primary loophole in campaign finance law that both parties exploited.

In their zeal to raise large amounts of this money, both parties offered donors a range of perks for giving. The Democratic National Committee (DNC) offered annual memberships in a fund-raiser's Executive Council to contributors giving $100,000. For their annual contribution, members were given the opportunity to meet with party officials and "offer insight and provide leadership on issues facing the party and the country." Members were also "accorded Honored Guest status at all DNC events, including the Democratic convention."

To their contributors, the Republican National Committee (RNC) offered membership in the committee's Team 100 club at the price of $100,000 to join, another $100,000 every fourth year after joining, and $25,000 in the years between. Benefits of a Team 100 membership include the opportunity to attend national and regional meetings with the Republican leadership and elected officials, international Team 100 business missions, and tickets to the committee's annual gala and the 1996 Republican convention.

A breakdown of donor soft money contributions for both parties reveals the pattern presented in Figure 5.2. Democrats received approximately 87 percent of their soft money from business and 11 percent from organized labor.[12] Republicans received 96 percent of their contributions from business and only 1 percent from labor.

Top ten soft money donors of $150,000 or more to the Democratic National Committee are shown in Table 5.2. Top ten soft money donors of $175,000 or more to the Republican National Committee are shown in Table 5.3. Many of these same organizations, along with other large donors, gave money to both parties. A listing of twenty top donors ($150,000 or more) to both parties shows this to be the case (see Table 5.4).

Of the total $263.5 million, the RNC received $141.2 million and the DNC received $122.3 million. Both parties spent the major share on "issue ads." These were primarily television ads either promoting the party leaders and incumbents or attacking the opposition. The ads, however, stopped short of expressly advocating the election or defeat of any candidates, thus exploiting a loophole in existing campaign laws. Because no spending limits existed on these issue ads, both parties spent heavily. The Democratic National Committee launched their ad campaign in the spring of 1996. Republicans began to counter with their ads in late summer.

What does all this money "buy"? Do the aforementioned donors or players inevitably receive special tax breaks, a reduction in government regulations, or a specific subsidy? Usually not in the short run. These contributions are usually made without an explicit quid pro quo. There is a general understanding that the contributor is satisfied with the party's good judgment on issues of common concern.

FIGURE 5.2   Soft Money Contributions by Sector

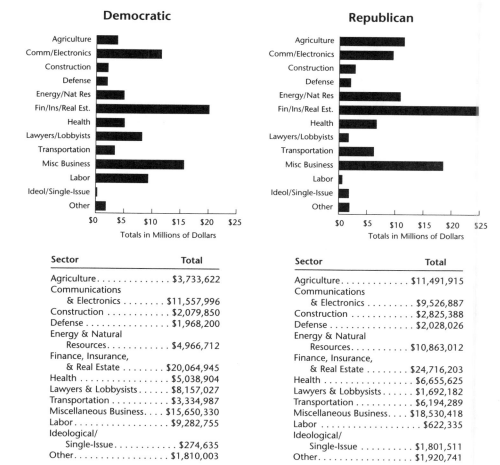

Sector	Total
Agriculture	$3,733,622
Communications & Electronics	$11,557,996
Construction	$2,079,850
Defense	$1,968,200
Energy & Natural Resources	$4,966,712
Finance, Insurance, & Real Estate	$20,064,945
Health	$5,038,904
Lawyers & Lobbyists	$8,157,027
Transportation	$3,334,987
Miscellaneous Business	$15,650,330
Labor	$9,282,755
Ideological/ Single-Issue	$274,635
Other	$1,810,003

Sector	Total
Agriculture	$11,491,915
Communications & Electronics	$9,526,887
Construction	$2,825,388
Defense	$2,028,026
Energy & Natural Resources	$10,863,012
Finance, Insurance, & Real Estate	$24,716,203
Health	$6,655,625
Lawyers & Lobbyists	$1,692,182
Transportation	$6,194,289
Miscellaneous Business	$18,530,418
Labor	$622,335
Ideological/ Single-Issue	$1,801,511
Other	$1,920,741

Source: Press release from the Center for Responsive Politics, "Soft Money to Parties Tripled Since 1992," February 17, 1997.

TABLE 5.2 Top Ten Soft Money Donors of $150,000 or More to the Democratic National Committee

Contributors	Democrats	Totals	Industry
Joseph E. Seagram & Sons[a]	$1,261,700	$1,938,845	Beer, wine, and liquor
American Federation of State, County, Municipal Employees[a]	1,134,962	1,134,962	Public sector unions
Communications Workers of America[a]	1,130,300	1,130,300	Industrial unions
Walt Disney Co.[a]	1,063,050	1,359,500	Media/Entertainment
Food and Commercial Workers Union[a]	727,550	727,550	Miscellaneous unions
Laborers Union[a]	627,088	634,588	Building trade
Lazard Freres and Co.	624,500	787,600	Securities and investments
Revlon Group Inc./ MacAndrews and Forbes	623,250	763,250	Misc. manufacturing and distributing
MCI Telecommunications Corp.[a]	607,296	964,514	Telephone utilities
Association of Trial Lawyers of America[a]	606,300	803,400	Lawyers/Law firms

[a]Includes more than one contributor affiliated with an organization.

TABLE 5.3 Top Ten Soft Money Donors of $175,000 or More to the Republican National Committee

Contributor	Republicans	Totals	Industry
Philip Morris[a]	$2,520,518	$3,017,036	Tobacco
R.J.R. Nabisco[a]	1,188,175	1,442,931	Tobacco
Atlantic Richfield[a]	764,471	1,250,843	Oil and gas
Joseph E. Seagram & Sons[a]	677,145	1,938,845	Beer, wine, and liquor
News Corp.[a]	654,700	654,700	Media/Entertainment
Brown and Williamson Tobacco	635,000	642,500	Tobacco
American Defense Institute	600,000	600,000	Foreign and defense policy
U.S. Tobacco Co.[a]	556,603	674,965	Tobacco
AT&T	552,640	974,524	Telephone utilities
Enron Corp.[a]	544,500	686,900	Oil and gas

[a]Includes more than one contributor affiliated with an organization.

Large contributors, though, do expect to be able to call or visit with sympathetic public officials and present their views and/or concerns. On the congressional level, major donors expect to meet or speak directly to certain party and legislative leaders. They also expect more immediate and direct responses from members of Congress than do noncontributors. At the White House level, major contributors may or may not get to speak with the president or vice president. But they do at least expect to communicate their views to high-level White House personnel or cabinet officials.

TABLE 5.4 Top Twenty Donors of $150,000 or More to Both the Republican and Democratic Parties

Contributor	Totals	Democrats	Republicans	Industry
Philip Morris[a]	$3,017,036	$ 496,518	$2,520,518	Tobacco
Joseph E. Seagram and Sons	1,938,845	1,261,700	677,145	Tobacco
R.J.R. Nabisco	1,442,931	254,756	1,188,175	Tobacco
Walt Disney Co.[a]	1,359,500	1,063,050	296,450	Media/Entertainment
Atlantic Richfield[a]	1,250,843	486,372	767,471	Oil and gas
AT&T	974,524	422,184	552,340	Telephone utilities
Federal Express	973,525	592,625	380,000	Air transport
MCI Telecommunications	964,514	607,296	357,218	Telephone utilities
National Education Association[a]	875,735	426,600	449,135	Public sector unions
Association of Trial Lawyers of America	803,400	606,300	197,100	Lawyers/Law firms
Lazard Freres and Co.[a]	787,600	624,500	163,100	Securities and investments
Anheuser-Busch[a]	726,107	401,107	325,000	Beer, wine, & liquor
Eli Lilly and Co.	746,835	238,850	506,985	Pharmaceutical/ Health products
Time Warner[a]	725,250	401,250	325,000	Media/Entertainment
Chevron Corp.	702,306	176,050	526,256	Oil and gas
Archer-Daniels-Midland[a]	700,000	295,000	405,000	Agri. service/products
NYNEX Corp.[a]	651,602	240,347	411,255	Telephone utilities
Textron Inc.	648,000	274,700	373,300	Defense aerospace
Northwest Airlines[a]	584,445	327,400	257,045	Air transport
Energy Corp.[a]	581,975	295,000	286,975	Electric utilities

[a]Includes more than one contributor affiliated with an organization.

CAMPAIGN FINANCE REFORM: SOME CAVEATS

Campaign reform legislation passed in the 1970s was intended to eliminate the assumed corruptive influence of large donors and replace it with a system composed of small, individual donors. Underlying this legislation was the concept that a relatively broader base of contributors would produce a more representative and public-regarding system of electoral advocacy. As this data illustrates, this has not turned out to be the case.

The rise of PACs and their activities are an unintended consequence of the aforementioned reform legislation. PACs grew out of an existing tension in American politics between reformist ideals about how interests ought to be organized, represented, and involved in elections and what interests actually do get represented in electoral processes.

Unfortunately, much so-called reform legislation occurs in the aftermath of political scandals—Teapot Dome and Watergate, for example. In these cases, there was a general assumption that widespread governmental corruption existed. In response, generally enacted restraints on the existing system enforced a leveling of what legitimate donations were and were not. The idea was to diminish the assumed corruptive influences through an established restraining system as far as political donations were concerned. Implicit in all this are the earlier tenets of turn-of-the-century progressivism that sought to purge American politics of bossism, corruption, partisanship, and other activities that smacked of special interest influences.

Much of the current discussion of campaign reform—in law journals, court decisions, legislative debates, and so on—concerns campaign spending limits. The assumption here is that unequal contributions lead to unequal representation for donors; that is, the greater the contribution, the greater the political access and/or political influence.

The growing involvement of soft money in American elections is increasingly bothersome to many private and public citizens. As noted earlier, hundreds of millions of soft money dollars were solicited and spent by both major parties in the most recent presidential election. Congress, for example, already is considering regulatory legislation with respect to the involvement of soft money in future elections. Some examples introduced in the 105th Congress are presented in Box 5.1. At this point, no one knows what the content will finally be.

Is viewing campaign finance as the locus of interest group power with respect to electoral outcomes a distorted view? Are most interest groups interested in elections? Are those that establish PACs usually able to raise large amounts of money that lead to influence? Are restraints necessary on PAC spending? There are no easy answers to these and other questions. Many interest groups avoid elections, preferring to use other tactics such as administrative and/or legislative lobbying. A loose coalition of citizens may

**BOX 5.1   Examples of Legislation to Regulate Soft Money
Introduced in the 105th Congress**

Senate

S.25   Sens. John McCain (R-Ariz.) and Russell Feingold (D-Wis.). Sets vol-
           untary spending limits and bans PAC contributions in Senate elec-
           tions; bans soft money gifts.

House

H.R. 97   Rep. Frederick Upton (R-Md.). Bars former lawmakers from lobby-
           ing for foreign governments.

H.R. 99   Rep. Rick White (R-Wash.); H.R. 141 Rep. John Dingell (D-Mich.);
           H.R. 170 Rep. Bob Franks (R-N.J.). Established a temporary com-
           mission to recommend campaign finance reforms.

H.R. 110   Rep. Bob Clement (D-Tenn.). Bans soft money to influence federal
           elections.

H.R. 138   Rep. Jay Dickey (R-Ark.). Bans PAC contributions to federal candi-
           dates.

H.R. 179   Rep. William Goodling (R-Pa.); H.R. 181 Rep. Porter Goss (R-Fla,).
           Proposes numerous campaign finance reforms.

H.R. 187   Rep. Alice Hasting (D-Fla.). Establishes commission to recommend
           the size of the House and the method for electing its members.

H.R. 223   Rep. Bill McCollum (R-Fla.). Establishes a presidential debate com-
           mission; reduces taxpayer funding for the nominating conventions
           of political parties whose candidates refuse to debate.

Source: From *Political Finance & Lobby Report,* (Arlington, VA: Amward Publishers) XVIII, January 29,
     1997, p. 4.

be unsure of where their political interests lie and may avoid involvement in
the electoral process. Or existing campaign restrictions may hamper new
organizations or numbers of small citizen action organizations. The point is
that today's campaign legislation is not content neutral. Organizationally
disadvantaged groups must construct and maintain ad hoc coalitions of
individual and institutional donors, whereas organizationally advantaged
groups (e.g., business and profit organizations) can employ their vast institutional powers to mobilize and channel their resources in whatever ways
the laws allow.

In his study of political action committees and campaign contributions, Thomas Gais notes an existing bias:

Limits on the maximum size of contributions—as well as their institutional resources—inhibit citizen interests and interests typically represented by professionals in the nonprofit sector from participating in elections and thus restrict "the number of issues discussed" and the depth of their exploration.[14]

Gias goes on to argue that legal constraints on both the size and sources of contributions diminish the expression of certain interests no less than limits on expenditures. Applying a single restrictive law to all types of interest contributions, in Gais's opinion, violates First Amendment speech protections.

Further, does today's PAC universe control so much money that it is disproportionately represented within the national interest group system? Note Table 5.5. Although these amounts of PAC money may be intimidating, they do not tell the whole story as far as campaign spending is concerned. One must also factor in money from such sources as liaison and public affairs offices within corporations, public law firms, research organizations, think tanks, Washington law firms, and individual donors. If one could total the sums spent by these entities, PACs constitute only a small piece of the political interest group universe by comparison, and dollar amounts solicited and spent by them is relatively minuscule compared to the amounts of money spent on all forms of interest group advocacy.

Improved public disclosure could serve as a restraint on large corporate donations. The large corporate donations uncovered during the Watergate hearings demonstrated the need for full disclosure. If, indeed, this were to come about, then it is possible that large donations by business and industry would be restrained, given their need to maintain good relationships with customers, stockholders, and public officials.

TABLE 5.5   PAC Contributions: Incumbents, Challengers, Open Seats (millions of dollars)

	Incumbents		Challengers		Open Seats	
1995–1996	$146.4	67%	$31.6	15%	$39.8	18%
1993–1994	137.2	72%	19.0	10%	33.4	18%
1991–1992	135.3	72%	22.9	12%	30.7	16%
1989–1990	125.8	79%	16.2	10%	17.7	11%
1987–1988	118.2	74%	18.9	12%	22.2	14%
1985–1986	96.2	69%	19.9	14%	23.8	17%

Source: Campaigns and Elections, June 9, 1997, p. 14.

Presently, we do not have this sort of disclosure. Savvy and aggressive businesses funnel their money, not through PACs, but through contributions made directly to candidates and political parties in the form of soft money. Through this process, the public is kept in the dark, and weaknesses in the existing campaign legislation do not require candidate organizations to fully disclose donor identity. But if disclosure laws were strengthened and enforced, they could serve as an effective filter for campaign contributions.

It is, of course, rational to argue that elections must be insulated from the corrupting effects of money and its distorting influence. Therefore, limits on the size of individual contributions to political organizations when those organizations are involved in campaigns and elections are viewed as reasonable. The argument goes that elections play a vital role in democracies because they allow citizens to elect their leaders, and the vote is a resource available to all adult citizens.

But because campaigns and elections are so central to our democratic processes, because they command so much public interest and discussion, and because so much conflict and competition are intrinsic to their operations, they must remain open to various points of view and subject to attempts to influence that point of view. This need for openness, then, argues that deregulation is the way to go rather than increased regulation. Regulatory laws might be better applied to executive or administrative lobbying where issues and institutional arrangements are more likely to produce fewer debates by a highly skewed set of players. Many of the issues handled in this context can have a wide-ranging impact for many citizens.

Reform laws that many citizens believed would give them greater control over their representatives have not proved successful. Rather, this legislation has increased the safety of incumbents by doing away with a private campaign finance system that potentially could provide for greater candidate accountability. What we have today is a bewildering, decentralized system catering to a small segment of the interest group universe.

NOTES

1. See, for example, Elizabeth Drew, *Money and Politics: The New Road to Corruption* (New York: Macmillan, 1983); Philip M. Stern, *Still the Best Congress Money Can Buy* (Washington, DC: Regnery Gateway, 1992); Dan Clawson, Alan Neustadtl, and Denise Scott, *Money Talks: Corporate PACs and Political Influence* (New York: Basic Books, 1992); Henry Chappell, "Campaign Contributions and Congressional Voting" *Review of Economics and Statistics* 62, 1980, 77–83; Theodore Eismeier and Phillip H. Pollack, *Money, Business and the Rise of Corporate PACs in*

American Politics (New York: Quorum Books, 1988); and Gary Jacobson, *Money in Congressional Elections* (New Haven, CT: Yale University Press, 1980).

2. John R. Wright, *Interest Groups in Congress: Lobbying, Contributions and Influence* (Boston: Allyn and Bacon, 1996), p. 118.
3. Congressional Quarterly, *Dollar Politics: Issue of Campaign Spending* (Washington, DC: Congressional Quarterly Press, 1971), p. 27.
4. 424 U.S. 1 (1976).
5. Frank Sorauf, "Political Action Committees in American Politics: An Overview," in *What Price PACs?* (Washington, DC: Twentieth Century Fund, 1984), pp. 41–42.
6. See Thomas Gais, *Improper Influence: Campaign Finance Law, Political Interest Groups, and the Problem of Equality* (Ann Arbor: University of Michigan Press, 1996), pp. 88–95.
7. Ibid., p. 138.
8. Ibid., p. 158.
9. Frank Sorauf, "Who's in Charge?: Accountability in Political Action Committees," *Political Science Quarterly* 99 (1984), 595.
10. Quoted in the *Washington Post,* August 10, 1980.
11. John Daly and Jennifer Keen, "Soft Money of Parties Tripled Since 1992," press release (Washington, DC: Center for Responsive Politics, February 17, 1997).
12. Ibid.
13. Gais, op. cit., p. 176.

6

Lobbying Congress

Some General Observations

INTRODUCTION

Legislative lobbying was briefly discussed in Chapter 4. This chapter addresses in greater detail the nature and performance of Congress with respect to interest group lobbying. Both the nature and performance mechanisms of Congress play important roles in determining lobbying success or failure. A few caveats are helpful in this regard:

- Congress is a fundamentally fragmented and decentralized institution with political influence widely dispersed among its members.
- Congressional parties are essentially weak and unable to serve as centralizing forces as far as policymaking is concerned.
- Today's Congress is relatively more open to outside pressures such as interest groups, the executive, the courts, and the public at large.
- Legislative policymaking is often slow and difficult. Decision making frequently involves small increments rather than bold new programs.[1]

These attributes, both individually and collectively, largely determine interest group access and influence. The weakness of legislative parties, for example, offers more opportunities for interest groups to highlight issues for congressional consideration. Furthermore, because legislative decision making is slow and difficult, the chances for status quo organizations are enhanced.

All interests must factor into their strategies the decentralized character of Congress and its unique policymaking structures and procedures.

CONGRESS AS A POLITICAL SYSTEM

The best way to comprehend interest group interaction with Congress is to perceive the national legislature as a political system (see Fig. 6.1). As noted, Congress receives inputs from a number of outside sources. Many interest groups (e.g., farmers, veterans, environmentalists, senior citizens) lobby for enactment of legislation on their behalf (see Chapter 4). Of course, these claims must be reconciled with those emanating from the White House or various intermittent petitioners (e.g., the courts). These petitions are then processed through the various subsytems noted earlier, mainly committees or subcommittees. These function within a set of formal rules and procedures. Informal rules (rules pertaining to acceptable behavior) and practices contribute to the overall system's processes. The resulting congressional outputs are legislation, overview (legislative review of administrative agencies and their programs), and representation (responding to and promoting constituent demands).

Implicit in this discussion is the fact that the legislative process is dynamic. Feedback, as noted, is a process by which present outputs affect future congressional actions and outputs. What Congress does today affects what Congress will do tomorrow or next week. Legislative outputs can either satisfy or mollify some interests but disappoint others. The inability or unwillingness of Congress to deal with national crises (e.g., a recession) or other important issues (e.g., raising the minimum wage) can alienate various interests or the White House or the public at large, thereby weakening existing support systems. Feedback can also fuel changes in group strategies, requiring the expenditure of more institutional resources in order to change the status quo (e.g., strengthening gun control laws).

Finally, changes in the political environment can induce system changes such as the election of a new administration, a domestic or international crisis, or a controversial Supreme Court decision. The affected interests will undoubtedly direct a new set of inputs or demands to the Congress. Change is continuous, and the input–output processes of Congress remain constant.

Viewed within this context, varying combinations of interests operate through the legislative system availing themselves of the opportunities presented to them. Organized interests do not seek to undermine the legislative system but rather pursue their goals within the system. Additionally, interests approach members of Congress for purposes of changing their perceptions without discrediting the institution. Even when unsuccessful, rather than calling for drastic legislative changes, disappointed or ineffec-

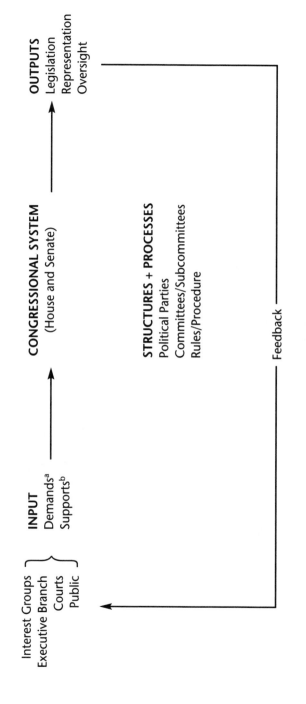

FIGURE 6.1 The Congressional System and Its Environment

Interest Groups
Executive Branch
Courts
Public

INPUT
Demands[a]
Supports[b]

CONGRESSIONAL SYSTEM
(House and Senate)

STRUCTURES + PROCESSES
Political Parties
Committees/Subcommittees
Rules/Procedure

OUTPUTS
Legislation
Representation
Oversight

Feedback

[a]Requests for certain benefits or policy decisions originating outside the Congress (e.g., interest groups, executives, the public, etc.).

[b]Maintenance of both a favorable and cooperative attitude toward the Congress by organized interests, the White House, and the public.

tive groups renew their struggle at some future time. In this fashion, legislative access is maintained, and the legitimacy of the legislative system is perpetuated.

We now turn to a number of internal changes in and elements of the legislative system that condition political access and policy influence. These include congressional membership, committees and subcommittees, congressional staffs, and legislative caucuses.

THE "NEW" CONGRESS

A new Congress functions today in place of the older Congress that existed at midcentury. This transformation has had important consequences for lobbying strategies and opportunities for policy influence.

The Congress of Sam Rayburn, Harry Byrd, Robert Taft, and Joe Martin no longer exists.[2] Or putting it differently, member composition of Congress is quite different from what it was in the forties, fifties, and early sixties. In the old Congress, a small but powerful elite monopolized the party leadership and committee chairs and generally ran the business of each chamber. This elite controlled the flow of legislation, negotiated with presidents, and dominated various committee and subcommittee routines. Life "on the Hill" was relatively slower, more personal, and more collegial. There was always time for a good story over a glass of bourbon in the late afternoon. Lobbyists and their organizations concentrated their efforts on this relatively small "inner club" of legislators. The rank-and-file were largely excluded.

But pressures for change began to build in the late sixties and early seventies. Congressional elections began to produce a "new breed" of politicians not awed by the hallowed traditions of Capitol Hill or by the effete "gentlemen's club" of the U.S. Senate.[3] Then-new members like Dale Bumpers, Richard Gephardt, Lowell Weicker, and Jacob Javits were elected on their own and not because they "paid their dues" to local or state party bosses. Characteristically, these new members were self-starters and policy oriented. They came to Capitol Hill to legislate—pass new environmental controls, expand civil rights, and enact more public regulatory controls on large corporations. The traditional niceties such as being seen and not heard and deferring to senior members had little attraction for them. The older norms or folkways described by Don Matthews over two decades ago no longer applied.[4] Junior members today have more chamber influence, more public visibility, and are more aggressive in their policy pursuits. As a result, the new Congress is less than the sum of its parts. With respect to lobbying influences in these changed circumstances, one source notes:

The many changes in Capitol Hill over the past decade—the proliferation of subcommittees, the greater importance of Congressional staff . . . the greater importance of policy entrepreneurs both among elected representatives and staff, the requirements for open meetings, the rapid turnover in Congressional membership—all of these things have altered the environment of legislative lobbying and left pressure groups bent on influencing officials with little choice but to escalate the range and volume of their activities.[5]

The electoral process has changed both the composition of Congress and its agenda. There are more interest group facilitators within the membership.[6] Issues like healthcare, welfare reform, and crime are high on today's legislative agenda. Advocates of these and other social issues have relatively greater potential for access and policy influence.

But what has just been stated should not imply that congressional members are totally tied to interest group influences. Today's legislators are much more sophisticated and knowledgeable with respect to lobbyists and their techniques. In addition, lawmakers retain a degree of independence because most remain electorally secure. In most cases, electoral defeat as a result of group opposition is extremely rare. Furthermore, when conflict exists involving many interests or coalitions thereof, many legislators can play one set of interests off against another. One source notes:

Groups turn to Congress as an institution where they can be heard, establish their positions, and achieve their policy goals. Members of Congress in turn rely on groups to provide valuable constituency, technical, or political information, to give reelection support and to assist strategically in passing or blocking legislation that the members support or oppose. Groups need Congress, and Congress needs groups.[7]

COMMITTEES AND SUBCOMMITTEES

Committees and Subcommittees, as the first step in drafting of legislation, are the frequent focii of intense lobbying pressures. Decisions reached here usually determine the contours and dynamics of subsequent lobbying efforts. A successful effort in committee, or subcommittee, can create a precedent and momentum for the floor debate. An unsuccessful lobbying effort makes it much more difficult to gain acceptance on the floor. Committee action is almost always the most important determinant of policy influence or failure.

In order to be effective, lobbies and lobbyists must have knowledge of how the various legislative subsystems work: politically, legislatively, and parliamentarily. For example: Is the committee chair a strong or weak advocate? Procedurally speaking, is the committee chair frequently confrontational or usually collegial? By nature, some committees split along partisan lines where others operate in a bipartisan fashion. With respect to the latter, the House Transportation and Infrastructure Committee (formerly Public Works and Transportation) is responsible for billion-dollar highway and construction projects and operates in a bipartisan manner. The committee doles out numerous capital improvement projects highly coveted by its members. On the other hand, House Banking and National Security Committee (formerly Armed Services) has a history of membership infighting with respect to national security goals.[8]

Further, it must be kept in mind that House and Senate committees have sharply different composition and rules. House committees are relatively larger and operate in a more partisan manner. Also, building a successful committee majority is more difficult than in the Senate. The Senate and its subsystems operate in more relaxed, less partisan manner. Each senator has the right of filibuster (unlimited debate to make a point). As a result, there are relatively greater efforts to reach consensus and accommodate senatorial preferences. Committee votes are rarely along strict party lines except for more partisan issues such as budget, certain presidential appointees, and some significant foreign policy issues.

A fruitful lobbying exercise within this subsystem requires the observance of a number of fundamentals,

- become acquainted with those legislators important to your organizational goals;
- know the committees of jurisdiction with respect to their personnel and procedures;
- anticipate organizational opposition;
- demonstrate a willingness to bargain and compromise at various points in the legislative process.

CONGRESSIONAL STAFFS AND LOBBYISTS

The process of lobbying various members of Congress usually involves congressional staff personnel. Given the increasing complexity of legislative issues, along with increasingly demanding work schedules, members of Congress heavily depend on staff. Today, over 20,000 staff members, researchers, budget analysts, and others are currently employed by Congress. Staff size has increased almost threefold since the sixties and early seventies. In addition, the staff size of committees and subcommittees has increased. State and district offices for Senators and House members are also substantial. State and district personnel serve as linkages to Washington offices in addition to providing service and casework.

Today, whether one speaks of the individual member's staff or those of committees, their role has evolved. Their duties go far beyond the traditional telephone answering, typing, filing, and duplicating. It is not uncommon for staff personnel to attend and advise members during committee or subcommittee hearings and later markups. Many have expertise in various policy areas (e.g., foreign policy, healthcare, finance, education, etc.). They are literally the "eyes," "ears," and even the "brain" of current members. Heavy travel and speaking demands on members literally force them to rely on staff for voting cues and information on upcoming bills and pending amendments. In addition, staff personnel draft legislation, conduct policy research, and indulge in a lot of parliamentary negotiation on behalf of their members as well as coalition building from time to time.

All of the foregoing highlights the importance of staff as far as lobbying is concerned. Political access, then, to staff personnel is of vital importance for lobbying success. Lobbyist interaction with these personnel can be every bit as important as talking to the elected official. This interaction, though, should not be a one-way street. As noted in an earlier chapter, rather than continuously making requests of congress members and their staffs, lobbyists can and do provide assistance and advice on occasion. A knowledgeable and experienced lobbyist has helpful information and contacts, and by making these available, valuable relationships are established. By offering such services as research, speech writing, and coalition building, opportunities for later political influence are enhanced.

LEGISLATIVE CAUCUSES AND COALITIONS

Virtually from the time of its establishment, Congress has contained a number of informal groups, coalitions, blocs, and caucuses. Today, well over 100 coalitions and caucuses function within the congressional membership. These structures demonstrate great variety and purpose and thereby reflect divergent interests within the membership.

Legislative caucuses vary in length of tenure, organizational sophistication, size, and ultimate policy influence.[9] Like their private counterparts, caucuses demonstrate fairly narrow as well as pluralistic goals. In addition to their representative function, the informal associations also indulge in information exchanges, policy development, and coalition building. Like their private counterparts, they seek to establish meaningful relationships with various sectors of the national bureaucracy (e.g., commerce, interior, agriculture, White House) for purposes of policy influence. Some recent and existing example of internal caucuses appear in Table 6.1.

TABLE 6.1 Congressional Caucuses and Coalitions

	House	Senate	Bicameral
Party	Democratic Study Group Republican Study Committee	Moderate/Conservative Democrats Wednesday Group	
Personal	Human Rights	Caucus on the Family	Arms Control and Foreign Policy
Interest	Space	Senators for the Arts	Renewable Energy Clearing House on the Future
Constituency Concerns			
National	Black Caucus Hispanic Caucus Sunbelt Council Textile Caucus		Caucus for Women's Issues Vietnam Veterans in Congress
Regional	Border Caucus Conference of Great Lakes Congressmen	Western States Coalition Midwest Conference of Democratic Senators Tennessee Valley Authority Caucus	Pacific Northwest Trade Task Force San Diego Congressional Delegation
State/District	Rural Caucus Federal Government Task Force House Caucus of North American Trade	Senate Caucus on North American Trade	Crime Caucus Committee on the Baltic States and Ukraine
State/District	Coal Group	Coal Caucus	Alcohol Fuels Caucus
Commercial	Port Caucus Steel Caucus Automotive Caucus	Cooper Caucus Rail Caucus Wine Caucus Tourism Caucus	Jewelry Manufacturing Coalition Wood Energy Caucus

State/district caucuses are noteworthy. Members representing districts in the same state recognize common interests such as securing harbor or shipping improvements, higher prices for farm commodities, or extra federal funding for capital improvements. These interests transcend party lines, with members of both parties consulting and pushing for the economic betterment of their constituents.

Caucuses can also provide advice on the substance of bills and cues about how to vote on amendments when both parties or some legislative committees are divided. Depending on the level of political activism and unity, a highly unified coalition or bloc can gain concessions from chamber leadership wanting certain legislation passed. The Congressional Black Caucus (CBC) has, in the past, successfully challenged the Democratic leadership in getting some of its preferred legislation passed by the House (e.g., extra funding for the District of Columbia government). Regardless of the stakes involved, these various associations add a dimension to the legislative system and thereby add another point of access in an already decentralized legislative institution.

Caucuses also maintain linkages with the various committees on issues of mutual concern (e.g., interstate commerce, crime, energy production, etc.) through their memberships. As a result, some issues and bills are addressed that might otherwise be stalled or buried in committee. Finally, caucus members derive electoral benefits as a result of their memberships because it allows linkages to a broader base of voters.

Interest group lobbying remains a persistent and central theme of today's legislative policymaking. Numerous associations of various political persuasion and makeup continue to approach Congress for diverse political favors or benefits. Despite earlier accounts and perceptions, organized interests do not regularly dominate the legislative process. Rather than decisive forces, interests groups should be perceived as one important source—but only one of many sources—seeking to influence the content of legislation. Not all petitioners are equally rewarded for their efforts. Congressional personnel have their own perceptions as to what the allocative decisions of Congress will be with respect to the petitioners. The centrality of organized interests in congressional decision making is not to be denied. Rather, their collective inputs must be kept in perspective, and many times this influence may be relatively more limited than publicly believed.

NOTES

1. Leroy N. Rieselbach, *Congressional Politics: The Evolving Legislative System,* 2nd ed. (Boulder, CO: Westview Press, 1995), p. xix.

2. An excellent source on the "old" Congress is William S. White, *Citadel: The Story of the U.S. Senate,* 2nd ed. (New York: Harper and Row, 1956).

3. Richard Bolling, *House Out of Order* (New York: Harper and Row, 1965) and Joseph Clark, *Sapless Branch* (New York: Harper and Row, 1964). Both authors describe the relative ineffectiveness of the "older" Congress.

4. Donald Matthews, *US Senators and Their World* (Chapel Hill: University of North Carolina Press, 1960).

5. John Tierney, testimony before the Senate Committee on Intergovernmental Affairs, quoted in *The Transformation in American Politics* (Washington, DC: Advisory Commission on Intergovernmental Relations, 1986), pp. 234–235.

6. Rieselbach, op. cit., p. 247.

7. Norman Ornstein and Shirley Elder, *Interest Groups, Lobbying and Policy Making* (Washington, DC: Congressional Quarterly Press, 1978), p. 224.

8. Bruce C. Wolpe and Bertram J. Levine, *Lobbying Congress: How the System Works,* 2nd ed., (Washington, DC: Congressional Quarterly Press, 1996), pp. 22–25.

9. See S.W. Hammond and A.G. Stevens, "Informal Congressional Caucuses and Agenda Setting," *Western Political Quarterly* 38, (1985), pp. 584–604.

7

Influencing the Executive

Actors and Strategies

INTRODUCTION

From both the individual and collective standpoint, the federal bureaucracy is comprised of many important interests in the policy game. There are dozens of departments, bureaus, commissions, government corporations, and the president. Many of their organizational charts do not show it, but numerous formal and informal arrangements exist within these agencies granting certain interests access to policy. Almost 1000 advisory committees exist within the various agencies today, giving their respective members or clientele groups a unique degree of access and/or voice in agency deliberations. These settings allow for hundreds of semiofficial associations to bring together congressional personnel, agency bureaucrats, possibly White House personnel, and group spokespersons. These formalized relationships, then, allow for the sharing and formalization of policy concerns.

The Farm Bureau, for example, is continuously concerned with the Department of Agriculture's farm policy, as are members of Congress on the House and Senate agriculture committees. The same kind of interaction and triangular relationships can be said to involve other interests such as the Atomic Energy Forum and the Highway Users Federation for Safety and Mobility. The former represents commercial nuclear power interests before the Nuclear Regulatory Commission and the latter interacts with Department of Transportation personnel on behalf of both public and private transportation systems. These close and ongoing systems are characterized by the late Grant McConnell as "representing the conquest of segments of formal state power by private groups and associations."[1]

This chapter examines patterns of player–agency interaction for purposes of policy influence. First, a brief chronology of bureaucratic growth is presented to gain a fuller appreciation of the size and scope of today's federal bureaucracy. Second, a number of lobbying strategies are noted in light of the foregoing. Finally, group interaction with the presidency is discussed, along with the expanding role of the Office of Management and Budget (OMB) in policing agency rule making. This chapter will give one a better understanding of the web of relationships that help determine and condition the policy outputs of the executive branch.

BUREAUCRATIC GROWTH: SIZE AND SCOPE

The size and scope of today's federal bureaucracy result from a number of factors. The chronology of this growth can be discussed from the standpoint of three political phases: (a) the Progressive era, (b) the New Deal and World War II era, and (c) the Great Society era and its immediate aftermath.

At the turn of the twentieth century, the emergence of the Progressive era led not only to the establishment of a relatively more professional public service system, but also to new public responsibilities.[2] The passage, for example, of the Pure Food and Drug Act (1907) initiated public surveillance of the manufacturing, distribution, and sale of drugs and food. The Federal Reserve Act (1913) established a Federal Reserve Board (now commonly known as the Fed) that was responsible for initiating greater pubic–private cooperation in the business of banking. This was in reaction to previous "panics" (or recessions) that occurred in the 1880s and 1890s. Government now had relatively greater responsibility for overseeing the nation's banking business and its transactions.

The stock market crash of 1929 and the resulting national depression led to another spurt in the size and scope of the federal bureaucracy. Under Franklin Roosevelt's New Deal, a host of new agencies (sometimes called "alphabetocracy") was established, greatly increasing federal regulation of the nation's economy. To name but a few, the Securities and Exchange Commission (SEC) was given authority to regulate stock exchanges along with the sale of stocks in interstate commerce. The rigging of stock prices and the sales of fraudulent stocks contributed to the 1929 crash. The National Labor Relations Board (NLRB) was established in this period to bring about improved management–labor negotiations with respect to unionization and bargaining over wages. The Civil Aeronautics Board (CAB) was established in 1938 (it is now defunct) to regulate competition along with air fares and freight rates in the fledgling airline industry. These and other New Deal agencies were generally responsible for bringing some level of growth and stability to the nation's economy. All of this was radically altering the national government's role in the lives of American citizens. The late V. O. Key states:

> [The national government] had been a remote authority with a limited range of activity. It operated the postal system, improved rivers and harbors, maintained the armed forces on a scale fearsome only to banana republics, and performed other functions of which the average citizen was hardly aware. Within a brief time, it became an institution that affected the lives and fortunes of most, if not all, citizens.[3]

The expansion that occurred with respect to the Great Depression was quickly followed by similar growth in connection with America's involvement in World War II. Soon after the declaration of war against the Axis powers (Germany, Italy, and Japan) President Roosevelt established a War Production Board. This ad hoc body was responsible for converting the nation's economy from peacetime to war. Instead of producing automobiles, refrigerators, and other civilian needs, the nation's factories began turning out airplanes, tanks, ammunition, and guns. In addition, there was governmental rationing of various material needed for the war effort such as gas and oil, food, and clothing. Further governmental entities were set up to enforce rent, wage, and price controls. These and other activities contributed to unprecedented levels of governmental involvement in and regulatory authority over the economy.

The politics of the sixties and seventies witnessed another spurt in the size and scope of the national bureaucracy in response to the consumer movement, the environmental movement and the women's movement. New agencies like the Environmental Protection Agency, the Consumer Product Safety Commission (CPSC), and the Equal Employment Opportunity Commission (EEOC) were established in response to citizen complaints of sex discrimination, false advertising claims by corporations, and the need to reduce levels of existing air and water pollution throughout the country.

This new generation of agencies differs from their predecessor with respect to their regulatory authority. Their jurisdiction extends to all public and private concerns. The EEOC's authority, for example, extends to both public and private concerns with respect to hiring, pay, promotions, and grievance procedures. Violations of these regulations can lead to litigation and fines.

Implicit here is the fact that Washington took on sweeping new responsibilities with respect to civil rights, the environment, health, and public safety. Its agenda now includes responsibilities that traditionally fell to the private sector. Washington's decision to shoulder these and other obligations and to right traditional wrongs has the ultimate effect of granting unprecedented policy discretion to a new generation of bureaucrats and agencies. Agency personnel are frequently left to interpret and write new regulations with little statutory guidance.

STRATEGIES OF INFLUENCE

Now that we have a clearer picture of the growing importance of the federal bureaucracy, what types of strategies exist for those interests desiring input? The quest can involve several strategies: lobbying, participation in executive appointments, agency adjudication, and participation in "advisory committee" activities. Depending on both the agency and the issues at hand, a combination of strategies may be utilized or a single approach may suffice.

Lobbying: Direct and Indirect

Lobbying the bureaucracy involves a number of activities such as monitoring regulatory agencies' new rulings or modifications of rulings, providing testimony and information during administrative hearings, and monitoring the performance of certain agencies on behalf of group members. Agency clientele may also hold press conferences, undertake advertising campaigns, and solicit media support to "build a fire" under wavering or recalcitrant policymakers. In addition, lobbyists occasionally undertake the sponsorship of test cases of administering regulations on behalf of affected interests.

An example of *direct* lobbying vis-à-vis the federal bureaucracy involves the Federal Trade Commission's attempts to regulate cigarette advertising. Established in 1914, the Federal Trade Commission (FTC) was established too prevent "unfair methods of competition in commerce." Its powers were broadened in 1938 to include regulation of "unfair or deceptive practices in commerce." This authority was reaffirmed by the Supreme Court in 1972.

In March 1964, in the wake of the surgeon general's report on the effects of smoking on health, the FTC proposed to issue a ruling mandating a warning on all packs and advertisements of cigarettes.[4] Three days of hearings were held by the commission with lobbyists for various cigarette manufacturers in attendance. Going into the hearings, four of the five commissioners favored a strong health warning on cigarettes, but the fifth, from North Carolina, a tobacco-producing state, favored negotiation on any kind of advertising. Some 2 months after the hearings, the FTC proposed a rule that all cigarette packages and advertising should carry the warning, "Cigarette Smoking Is Dangerous to Health and May Cause Death from Cancer and Other Diseases." Throughout the FTC's hearings, the cigarette industry argued that only Congress, and not the FTC, had the authority to legislate. The FTC, it claimed, was exceeding its authority.[5] Lobbying pressures, as a result, were directed toward members of Congress and committees that had responsibility for writing any type of legislation as contained in the FTC's statement. Nearly a quarter of all committees in the Senate and a third of all those in the House came from tobacco-producing states. Tobacco lobbyists indicated a willingness to accept some type of warning, but not one as strong as the FTC's.

To circumvent the enactment of any punitive legislation with respect to tobacco advertising, Earle Clements was hired as chief lobbyist and strategist. Clements was a former U.S. senator from Kentucky, a tobacco-producing state. Clements had worked very closely with Lyndon Johnson when the latter was majority leader in the Senate. Clements's well-established ties gave him a good deal of leverage in drafting tobacco legislation. His strategy was twofold. First was to come forward with some kind of warning that would mollify public concerns in the wake of the surgeon general's report. Second, in exchange for the warning, the FTC was barred from regulating tobacco advertising in the future. This essentially is what became law. When President Johnson signed the legislation, a mild health warning was to be included in labeling ("Caution, Cigarette Smoking May Be Hazardous to Your Health"), and no warnings were necessary on advertisements. There was also preemption that neither the FTC nor the Communications Commission (responsible for television advertising) would take any action for 3 years (the original language called for a permanent ban on the FTC and the Communications Commission). Tobacco lobbying paid off to a degree because the FTC's active role was muted, and cigarette consumption was not seriously threatened. On the other hand, *The New York Times* called the new law:

> A shocking piece of special-interest legislation ... a bill to protect the economic health of the tobacco industry by freeing it from proper regulation.[6]

The Federal Aviation Administration (FAA) is an example of an agency that approaches Marver Bernstein's model of a coopted system. In 1958, President Eisenhower signed the Federal Aviation Act that created the Federal Aviation Agency, which became the Federal Aviation Administration in 1983. In its creation, Congress saddled the agency with dual missions that affect its performances to this day. The agency's first mission was to regulate the burgeoning airline carriers. The second has been to promote the well-being of the industry. As a result, the FAA has demonstrated a good deal of reluctance to closely monitor and pressure various air carriers to maintain their equipment and constantly upgrade passenger services and safety.

The FAA's critics refer to it as the "tombstone" agency, implying that it acts only after there has been a fatal airline crash. Additionally, charges are made that it drags its feet on recommendations from the National Transportation Safety Board (NTSB) for the inspections of aircraft, closer monitoring of "bogus" parts installed on aircraft, and reconsideration of seating arrangements in aircraft that enhance survival in case of a crash. The prevailing attitude of the airline industry is that saving lives is not cost effective.

In a recent and rather exhaustive study of the airline industry and the role of the FAA as a public regulator, the Center for Public Integrity found an "incestuous" relationship between the agency and its clientele air carriers. The center's report notes, in part:

> [T]he FAA's cozy relationship with the airlines it regulates compromises the agency's Civil Enforcement Program. The Transportation Department's Office of the Inspector General found that the FAA's practice of allowing airlines to pay the costs of training FAA Flight inspectors "tend[s] to preclude FAA enforcement action on specific aircraft, airmen, and even the air carrier, regardless of circumstances that typically would result in enforcement."[7]

The report further states that thirty-one of the nation's largest air carriers are funding the training of FAA flight inspectors. The report also refers to a "lobbying juggernaut" of over 800 lobbyists active on Capitol Hill comprised of many former members of Congress and numerous airline personnel. The lobbying effort is supplemented by millions of dollars from air carriers to legislators with key roles in airline safety matters.

The report concludes that airline safety standards are not set by either the Congress nor the FAA but by the industry itself. Further:

> It is apparent that the aviation interests have overwhelmed the supposedly objective decision-making process as it pertains to them. As a result, today, when it comes to airline safety, Congress is more responsive to aviation interests than to the broad public interest.[8]

Although the Clinton administration and some members of Congress are calling for more vigorous regulatory activity on the part of the FAA, important elements of its constituency are opposed. Aircraft manufacturers, pilot unions, and some air carriers recently established a new organization, the Commercial Aviation Strategy Team, to mute criticisms of the agency and oppose reforms. This new organization is not totally opposed to policy modification, but it supports only those compatible with airline preferences.

As just noted, bureaucratic agencies differ with respect to their responses to interest group lobbying. These range from opposition to willing cooperation to virtual interest dominance. By and large, agencies respond selectively to salient demands from their petitioners as best suits their administrative and political needs.

Agencies themselves indulge in lobbying from time to time. When threatened by legislation aimed at reducing its regulatory authority, the Federal Trade Commission, for example, coordinated communications, provided relevant materials, and participated in periodic strategy sessions with its constituency. In the words of a former commissioner:

> Through our press office, we made certain that factual documents reached the hands of any reporter, columnist, or editorial writer who might wish to be informed of the commission's plight.[9]

A recent *indirect* or grass-roots approach with respect to the EPA and its policymaking is being mounted by Citizens for a Sound Economy (CSE). In October 1996, the CSE, a 250,000-member grass-roots lobby, mounted a $5-million multiyear campaign aimed at easing a number of the EPA's regulations on small businesses.[10] It launched an ad campaign in California, Michigan, and Washington, D.C., where proenvironmental groups are quite active and politically visible. It also produced and is disseminating in these and other states a half-hour television ad and forty-four-page magazine touting a more decentralized environmental regulatory system that gives states and localities authority and allows local businesses more flexibility in meeting standards. The CSE has hired a number of field directors to coordinate work in key grass-roots districts. A good deal of these lobbying expenses are being underwritten by powerful Washington-based lobbies like the National Association of Manufacturers, the American Petroleum Institute, and the Chemical Manufacturers Association.

Bureaucratic Appointments

High-level *bureaucratic appointments* offer another approach for concerned interests to influence public policy. Environmentalists, consumers, business associations, feminists, and so on want supportive appointees in policy sensitive positions throughout the executive structure.* Some of former Presi-

---

*During the early formation of the Bush administration, for example, organizations like the Heritage Foundation, the Chamber of Commerce of the United States, a coalition of eighty women's organizations, conservative religious orders, and environmental groups submitted thousands of resumes of individuals these various organizations wanted appointed to certain administrative posts.

dent Reagan's appointments are a case in point. Ms. Marjorie Mecklenberg was chosen to head the Office of Adolescent Pregnancy Programs at the Department of Health and Human Services. Prior to her selection, Ms. Mecklenberg was a member of and active in a number of antiabortion organizations. John B. Crowell served as legal counsel to timber interests bitterly opposed to existing policies concerning logging quotas. James B. Watt, chosen to be Secretary of Interior, came from the conservative Mountain States Legal Foundation.

Mr. Watt was brought into the Reagan administration to provide "regulatory relief" for elements of the Reagan constituency, especially smoke-emitting industries, and to blunt the existing body of environmental laws passed by Congress in the late 1960s and early 1970s. Proenvironmental organizations like Sierra, Friends of the Earth, World Wildlife Federation, and others perceived this appointment as environmentally hostile and saw the intended regulatory "reforms" as the cutting edge of a massive administrative assault on the institutional foundations of federal environmental laws. During the 1980s, these latter organizations expended a good deal of their resources defending the administrative and legislative achievements of the previous decade from this onslaught. Characteristic of many Reagan appointees was an antipathy toward the very programs these individuals were chosen to administer.

The confirmation process itself offers opportunities for group input. In 1975, for example, during senatorial confirmation hearings for Secretary-designate Stanley Hathaway, Senator Henry Jackson raised a series of questions dealing with Hathaway's policies on conflict-of-interest matters, the logging of outside contacts (maintaining a record of contacts by various lobbyists), and the leasing of public lands. These questions were submitted to the senator by Common Cause.[11] Jackson directed the nominee to respond, and these were inserted in the Interior Committee's confirmation report and constituted a pubic commitment on Hathaway's part. This procedure is not uncommon in other administrative confirmations.

Other Group Approaches

Administrative adjudication offers further opportunities for organized interests and players to impact administrative policymaking. When Congress creates a new department of agency such as the EPA, OSHA, or CPSC, it does so realizing that as legislators they do not have the time, the expertise, or the ability to involve themselves in administrative policymaking. The result, as we have seen, is that a good deal of policy discretion is left to federal bureaucrats. Policymaking, then, takes place on both formal and informal levels. Many decisions, for example, coming from the EPA are made daily by its staff personnel—identifying existing toxic waste dumps; issuing regulations concerning the labeling, storage, and disposal of pesticide containers; establishing emission standards for new motor vehicles; or setting noise levels that are acceptable for construction equipment (except aircraft), all motors and engines, and electronic equipment.

As an independent regulatory agency, the EPA has quasi- (or partial) legislative, administrative, and judicial functions. Not only does it draft regulations and procedures that bind its constituency—numerous proenvironmental organizations and many private concerns—but it enforces them as well. In this context, conflict over the content and purposes of proposed policies inevitably arises. To bring about compliance, the EPA and other regulatory agencies resort to administrative adjudication that resembles a trial. An agency-appointed judge conducts a hearing at which both sides present their claims. This process offers opportunities for clientele interests to press for certain policy modifications or initiatives. Additionally, almost all adjudicated cases allow for aggrieved parties to appeal to a federal circuit court. Adjudication, then, serves as a possible check on aggressive bureaucrats and their policy initiatives.

Finally, the existence of many *advisory committees* as semiofficial bodies within many executive agencies provides yet another set of players in the policy game. In their study of organized interests in Washington, Kay Schlozman and John Tierney found approximately 900 of these semiofficial bodies across the national bureaucracy.[12] The majority are comprised of representatives from corporations, business associations, labor unions, and citizens organizations. These bodies perform a number of important functions. First, the committees serve as a conduit for channeling pressures to agency policymakers. Second, this linkage also allows for the transmission of information to both sides (e.g., future agency plans, agency and governmental stands on issues of importance, interest group policy priorities, and internal processes of the agency). Finally, there is the ultimate goal of policy determination and implementation. Schlozman and Tierney note, for example, that an advisory committee within the old Social Security Administration played an important role in the shaping and implementation of the current Medicare program. In addition, the composition of the EPA's advisory committee was altered as a result of intensive "in-house" lobbying by tobacco interests.[13]

The foregoing discussion demonstrates a range of strategies available to interests pursuing administrative access and policy influence. Competition in this setting is often intense and confrontational because of the expanded size and scope of the federal bureaucracy (e.g., EPA bureaucrats being cross-pressured by environmentalists and fertilizer and pesticide producers or OSHA decision makers being pressured by labor and industrial interests). These situations do not usually lead to policy dominance but to policy accommodation.

THE WHITE HOUSE AND INTEREST GROUPS:
FROM TEMPORARY GUESTS TO PERMANENT RESIDENTS

As the modern presidency has come to play an increasingly important role in national policymaking, political interests groups perceive 1600 Pennsylvania Avenue as an important location in policy formation. Traditionally, most lobbyists spent more time on Capitol Hill, but today they are increasingly concerned with the presidency and its policymaking significance. The list of petitioners keeps getting longer. These include farmers, pro-lifers, feminists, the elderly, environmentalists, businesspeople, unionists, state and local officials, and so on.[14]

Presidential access, though, should not be viewed as a one-way street. Both sides have something to gain from these contacts. Presidents Roosevelt and Truman were lobbied by unionists and civil rights groups that supported many of the legislative initiatives of these presidents. Jewish and pro-Israeli organizations strongly lobbied Lyndon Johnson and Richard Nixon during the Arab–Israeli wars of the 1960s and 1970s. In return, they gave strong electoral support.

Presidents also receive other advantages for their group support. First, these interests can provide a sitting president with congressional support. These and other organizations can contact their congressional personnel with regard to certain House or Senate votes. Additionally, they can help presidents in their "intelligence gathering." This involves alerting the president and president's staff with regard to potential "firestorms" of opposition or to impending actions detrimental of administration goals. Finally, petitioning interests can build coalitions that generate great pressure on both congressional and administrative personnel for some kind of action.

As recently as Lyndon Johnson's administration, White House group interaction was on an ad hoc basis; many preferred to work through other administrative personnel and the president's personal staff. This type of interaction, though, became increasingly unsatisfactory for both sides.

As a result, the Office of Public Liaison (OPL) was established in 1974. This institutionalized access to the White House and the president. Access is now formalized between various presidential aides assigned to deal with these exchanges. Over time, the number of exchanges and personnel assigned has grown. Presidents Carter, Ford, and Reagan developed a growing number of OPL staffers who had "portfolio management responsibilities" with a range of interests such as Jews, farmers, consumers, the elderly, unionists, and so on.

Although this high level of access is important, some petitioners seek an audience with the president himself. In this context, the president hears the various claims in person, and the petitioners can exchange information with the president personally. Individual presidents, of course, have had their own hierarchy of preferences as far as group petitioners are concerned. By way of illustration, data are presented in Tables 7.1–7.4 contrasting the access differential between the Carter and Reagan administrations as far as interest groups were concerned.

As the data show, Carter gave disproportionate attention to blacks followed by Jews, feminists, and several other minorities. The black community comprised an important element in Carter's electoral victory, and contact with them continued into the term. Women, Greeks, and the elderly fared less well.

As Table 7.2 shows, black access to Reagan was much more restricted. The Hispanic community was an important element in Reagan's winning coalition in 1980, and he initially demonstrated his gratitude by granting access. But as time passed, access to Reagan became increasingly restricted. As one source notes:

> From July 1, 1982 to June 30, 1983 he [Reagan] met with only two minority groups. After his initial thanks for electoral support, the Reagan Administration became a place where minority groups could not lobby the president in person.[15]

This development was in keeping with Reagan's political rhetoric about being president for the people and not a president tied down to narrow minority interests. Incidentally, feminists who complained about limited access to Carter found that it was much better than they experienced under Reagan.

With respect to public policy orientations, again there is a clear contrast between group access to Carter and Reagan. Table 7.3 shows Carter's interaction with organizations as generally moderate to liberal. Labor union access was the highest, followed by veterans organizations. As a born-again Christian, Carter also met with religious groups more than twenty times. Those with relatively limited presidential access were representatives from business associations, bankers, and corporate leaders. Carter's interaction shows an up-and-down trend, but toward the end of his term, his interaction dropped off significantly.

Noting Reagan's interactions with interest groups (Table 7.4), one can see a pattern quite different from Carter's. Overall, Reagan met with corporate leaders more than with any other set of interests. His forty-two meetings with these interests demonstrate more structured access and not one of eliminating access. Multiple access was granted to a number of interests that were conservative or right wing. In further contrast to Carter, Reagan did not meet with any public interest groups, consumer, or environmental groups during this period. Interestingly, though, Reagan did grant access to a broader array of interests than did Carter.

TABLE 7.1 Carter Interaction with Minorities: 1977–1979 Meetings

	1st Half 1977	2nd Half 1977	1st Half 1978	2nd Half 1978	1st Half 1979	Totals
Blacks	4	8	4	10	4	30
Hispanics/ Latinos	3	0	0	0	0	3
Jews	1	1	1	0	1	4
Arabs	0	1	0	0	0	1
Native Americans	0	0	1	1	0	2
Greeks	0	0	1	0	0	1
Elderly	0	1	0	0	0	1
Women/ Feminists	1	1	0	1	1	4
Totals	9	12	7	12	6	46

Source: John Orman, "The President and Interest Group Access," *Presidential Studies Quarterly XVIII* (1988), p. 788.

TABLE 7.2 Reagan Interaction with Minorities: 1981–1983 Meetings

	1st Half 1981	2nd Half 1981	1st Half 1982	2nd Half 1982	1st Half 1983	Totals
Blacks	9	4	6	0	0	19
Hispanics/ Latinos	21	0	1	0	1	23
Jews	2	1	1	0	0	4
Polish	0	3	1	1	0	5
Italians	0	1	0	0	0	1
Ethnics unspecified	1	1	0	0	0	2
Elderly	0	1	0	0	0	1
Totals	33	11	9	1	1	55

Source: John Orman, "The President and Interest Group Access," *Presidential Studies Quarterly XVIII* (1988), p. 789.

TABLE 7.3   Carter Interaction with Interest Groups: 1977–1979 Meetings

	First Half 1977	2nd Half 1977	1st Half 1978	2nd Half 1978	1st Half 1979	Totals
Unions	12	6	13	2	2	35
Military/Vets	8	2	7	5	2	24
Arts/Humanities	1	0	1	2	0	4
Farmers	1	1	2	2	0	6
Small businesses	1	0	1	0	2	4
Bankers	2	0	0	0	0	2
Professional associations	5	1	1	1	0	8
Education	3	2	4	0	3	12
Corporate leaders	3	4	5	2	2	16
National business groups	1	1	5	0	1	8
Public Interest/Environmental	6	5	6	0	4	21
Religious	8	4	1	5	3	21
Totals	51	26	46	17	19	162

Source: John Orman, "The President and Interest Group Access," *Presidential Studies Quarterly XVIII* (1988), p. 790.

TABLE 7.4 Reagan Interaction with Interest Groups: 1981–1983 Meetings

	1st Half 1981	2nd Half 1981	1st Half 1982	2nd Half 1982	1st Half 1983	Totals
Unions	10	3	2	0	3	18
Military/Vets	2	1	8	0	3	14
Arts/Humanities	1	0	0	1	0	2
Farmers	15	1	1	0	0	17
Small businesses	0	1	3	1	1	6
Professional associations	1	2	1	0	2	6
Education	1	3	3	3	7	17
Corporate leaders	1	10	11	12	8	42
National business groups	5	2	1	1	1	10
Public interest/ environmental	0	0	0	0	0	0
Religious	2	9	1	4	5	21
Conservative/ Right wing	22	1	3	0	4	30
Totals	60	33	34	22	34	183

Source: John Orman, "The President and Interest Group Access," *Presidential Studies Quarterly XVIII* (1988), p. 790.

But in his campaign rhetoric, Reagan criticized a government run by interest groups, and as Mark Peterson and the late Jack Walker note:

> The Reagan administration believes that to permanently reduce the size of the federal government—-the president's fundamental, overriding goal—the number of interest groups must be reduced.[16]

Some lobbying tips with respect to the White House are listed in Box 7.1.

Box 7.1

1. Relate your issue or objective to the president's program if possible. Point out how it could support the program, and if it doesn't, think twice before taking it to the president.

2. Seek some common tie between the White House and your corporation, association, or other client. Same party? State ties? Common friends? Common goals? Campaign support?

3. Build cordial relationships with White House staff by extending offers to help support administrative objectives.

4. Invite White House staff to corporate meetings to speak and advise the President that his initiatives have helped the country and business.

5. Keep White House staff advised on industry developments and issues. (This only applies to major associations or corporations.) White House staff often requires more information than does Capitol Hill.

6. Know how the White House operates and the president's relationship with key cabinet members. Know who makes the decisions and prepares briefings and position papers. Every White House has a different operation.

7. Lobby to get your issue noted in a briefing or issue paper. If it doesn't get to the Oval Office or hasn't been discussed by staff, there is no chance for White House support.

8. Don't try to take any issue directly to the president.

Source: John L. Zorack, *The Lobbying Handbook: A Comprehensive Guide* (Washington, DC: Professional Lobbying and Consulting Center, 1990), p. 182.

THE ROLE OF THE OFFICE OF MANAGEMENT AND BUDGET

White House lobbying also entails touching base with the Office of Management and Budget (OMB). Created in 1970 (replacing the old Bureau of the Budget), this agency's authority extends beyond budgetary matters to those including the process of reviewing all legislative proposals from the executive agencies and agency rule making. As part of the OMB, a Legislative Reference Division (LRD) performs this function. Presidents depend on the LRD to fulfill the important responsibility of coordinating and executing "legislative clearances." This means that all legislation and every communication sent to Capitol Hill by executive agencies must coincide with the administration's policies. Any differences are reconciled through the OMB's clearinghouse with the president being the final arbiter. Legislative approval also applies to testimony by executive personnel before legislative committees and to any reporting that agencies submit to Congress on impending legislation. (This also applies to testimony by lobbyists before congressional committees.) The LRD contains a number of analysts, lawyers, and other legislative specialists who review agency requests along with those from other sources like Cabinet secretaries and their staffs. If the LRD's analysis determines that some of these bills have "policy implications," the White House is quickly informed.[17]

OMB's supervision of agency rule making (or regulatory authority) is equally important to lobbyists. The agency is a major watchdog over all the agencies in this regard. It functions to make sure that all "regulatory programs" are consistent with those of the president. OMB is comparable to the House Rules Committee in acting as the president's regulatory cop over intended regulatory rules. In submitting their annual regulatory agendas, agencies planning to draft certain regulations in their areas of jurisdiction must notify OMB. This allows for that agency to block or veto any rule-making processes that the White House does not approve of. (Of course, Congress has ultimate authority to draft subsequent legislation nullifying proposed agency guidelines.)

As one can see, OMB is a major participant in policy formation. For lobbyists to concentrate on the White House and ignore this agency can spell disaster for clients. Although lobbying OMB and the Congress can be somewhat similar, OMB is less susceptible to pressure. But for any lobbyist whose client has an interest in changing laws or modifying administrative regulations, approaching OMB personnel is essential.

This chapter has emphasized the fact that today's federal bureaucracy is a force in national policymaking. Political conflict does not end after Congress passes a bill and the president signs it. The struggle merely shifts to the bureaucracy. Bureaucratic power and expertise have grown with increases in the size of government, advances in technology, and the increasingly complex problems government must deal with today. Both the president and the Congress delegate a good deal of authority to various bureaus or departments that have more time and expertise to deal with these problems. Therefore, the bureaucracy fills in the gaps and interprets what newly passed laws mean. All of this is not lost on today's interest group universe. An increasing level of resources and attention is now devoted to approaching and convincing public officials at all levels (including the president) of the importance of their respective claims. How various public officials respond to these pressures can be quite unpredictable.

NOTES

1. Grant McConnell, *Private Power and American Democracy* (New York: Vintage Books, 1967), p. 162.
2. See Richard Hofstader, *The Age of Reform* (New York: Random House, 1955).
3. V. O. Key, *The Responsible Electorate* (New York: Random House, 1966), p. 31.
4. See Peter Taylor, *The Smoking Ring* (New York: Mentor Books, 1985).
5. Ibid., pp. 191–195.
6. *The New York Times,* May 4, 1969, p. 1.
7. *In the Unlikely Event: The Politics of Airline Safety* (Washington, DC: The Center For Public Integrity, 1998), p. 10.
8. Ibid., p. 4.
9. Michael Pertschuck, *Revolt Against Regulation: The Rise and Pause of the Consumer Movement* (Berkeley: University of California Press, 1982), p. 107.
10. *National Journal,* October 26, 1996, pp. 2297-2298.
11. Andrew McFarland, *Common Cause* (Chatham, NJ: Chatham House, 1984), p. 142.
12. Kay Schlozman and John Tierney, *Organized Interests and American Democracy* (New York: Harper and Row, 1986) pp. 333-334.
13. "Tobacco Group Lobbies EPA on Study Panel," *The New York Times,* October 22, 1990, p. A11.
14. See Thomas A. Cronin, *The State of the Presidency,* 2nd ed. (Boston: Little, Brown, 1980).
15. John Orman, "The President and Interest Group Access," *Presidential Studies Quarterly,* XVIII (1988), p. 788.
16. "The Impact of the First Reagan Administration upon the National Interest Group System," Paper presented at the American Political Science Association meeting, August 1985, p. 1.
17. John L. Zorack, *The Lobbying Handbook: A Comprehensive Guide* (Washington, DC: Professional Lobbying and Consulting Center, 1990), p. 195.

8

Courts and Policymaking

The Litigation Explosion

INTRODUCTION

After having traveled in the United States and observed its political processes, a young Frenchman wrote, "There is hardly a political question in the United States which does not sooner or later turn into a judicial one."[1] Although this observation was made more than 100 years ago, it is, if anything, truer today. The federal judiciary (including the Supreme Court), like the Congress and the president, is a leading participant today in deciding some of the more contentious issues in American politics:

- the elimination of segregated public schools
- the equality of representation in state and congressional districts
- the limits of free speech and press and of obscenity and censorship
- the rights of criminal defendants with respect to searches, questioning and access to legal counsel
- the right of a person to terminate one's life because of illness

Courts are political actors just like the bureaucracy and the Congress. Courts decide "who gets what" in our society. They also do not merely apply the law but are "the molders of policy rather than the impersonal vehicles of revealed truth."[2] Reflecting on the increased role of courts, one source notes:

> The courts have changed their roles in American life. American courts, the most powerful in the world—they were that when Tocqueville

wrote and when Bryce wrote—are now far more powerful than ever before.[3]

UNIQUENESS OF THE JUDICIAL SYSTEM

It is incorrect to assume that the procedures and processes of federal courts are similar to those of the other two branches of government. This uniqueness not only conditions the policy outcome of courts but affects lobbying strategies as well. With regard to *style,* courts do not initiate policy as do legislators or bureaucrats. Only through the process of litigation (bringing a series of suits before the courts) can judicial policy be established. Incidentally, most litigation does not produce new policies. Second is *access.* Interest groups may buttonhole a legislator in his or her office or off the floor but not so with judges. The petitioner must hire a lawyer and meet the requirement of "jurisdiction." The contending parties must have legal standing in the eyes of the court and be affected by the impending decision. Third, judicial *procedures* are quite different from those of the other two branches. The use, for example, of propaganda, public relations, or face-to-face lobbying has no place in court. Communications to the courts must be in the form of briefs or other documentation. Fourth, most decisions apply only to *the litigants bringing the suit.* Whereas Congress or the White House may announce broad new polices with respect to industrial pollution, social security increases, or international trade, courts address their findings to the parties in the suit. Finally, court processes must demonstrate *objectivity.* Both individuals and groups fully expect members of Congress to think of impartiality. Generally, too, judicial decisions do not lend themselves to the same degree of bargaining and compromise as occurs in the other two branches. Rather, court rulings are characterized by an intensive investigation of the facts and points of law. These procedures, however, do not preclude a good deal of interaction and case discussion among the judges themselves.

JUDICIAL STRATEGIES

In light of the foregoing, various organizations adopt their strategies accordingly. Of course, not all interests approach the third branch of government, but a number of strategies are available to those that do.

Litigation

Litigation represents a direct approach to influencing the federal judiciary. This is the process of bringing a series of suits before the courts to gain a favorable decision or policy determination. As a strategy, litigation is dependent on the availability of certain resources or capabilities. First, money is important because litigation can be quite expensive and time-consuming. Some suits, such as civil rights disputes, may entail several years of litigation. Second, the level of legal resources is important. Many of today's litigators have "in-house" legal talent to prepare for litigation and monitor other ongoing suits. Some organizations may merely join a suit being brought by other like-minded organizations. Further, if litigants have meaningful linkages to other federal personnel or agencies, those resources can be put into play.

Litigation is driven by other factors as well. When Congress, for example, enacts legislation such as environmental laws, voting rights, or affirmative action, legal interpretation in different settings (e.g., at the state or local level) is required. No law, regardless of how carefully drawn, can cover every eventuality. Courts, therefore, are actively involved in deciding what the law "really" means.

The Environmental Protection Agency (EPA) experiences this type of situation. Given a broad mandate of "cleaning up the environment," the EPA is responsible for many different aspects of environmental policymaking. Congress, however, does not have the requisite expertise in this and other areas when establishing an agency.[4] As a result, much of the early environmental legislation passed required a good deal of interpretation by both the agency itself and the courts. The ambiguity of legislation then opens the door for greater judicial involvement under the guise of interpretation.

Interest aggregations on the political left (e.g., women, environmentalists, and civil rights activists) petitioned the courts with increasing frequency in the 1970s and 1980s. In this context, one source notes interests,

> that are highly dependent upon the judicial process as a means of pursuing their policy interests do so usually because they are temporarily or even permanently, disadvantaged in terms of their abilities to attain successfully their goals in the electoral process, within the elected political institutions, or in the bureaucracy. If they are to succeed at all in the pursuits of their goals they are almost compelled to resort to litigations.[5]

Many court decisions in this period proved to be instrumental in advancing the goals of these groups such as expanded employment opportunities, equal pay for both sexes, and the establishment and maintenance of abortion rights. These interests were also facilitated by changes in the rules governing access to the courts (or standing).[*] Additionally, the federal

---

[*]Feminist organizations like NOW have instigated a number of class action suits before the courts with respect to claims of sex discrimination in hiring, pay, and promotions. Class action suits are suits initiated by parties acting on behalf of themselves and all others similarly situated.

judiciary contained activists who viewed federal intervention in socioeconomic matters as both desirable and appropriate.

With respect to abortion, for example, the high court's holding in *Roe* v. *Wade* set off an avalanche of litigation on both sides of the issue.[6] Highly visible pro-choice organizations in 1970s and 1980s litigation were Planned Parenthood, American Civil Liberties Union (ACLU), National Abortion Rights Action League (NARAL), Catholics for Free Choice, National Organization for Women (NOW), Religious Coalition for Abortion Rights, American Jewish Congress, and so forth. Leading pro-life organizations during this period were the National Conference of Catholic Bishops, Celebrate Life, League for Infants, Fetuses, and the Elderly, American Academy of Medical Ethics, Catholic Lawyers Guild, American Family Association, and American Life League.

Litigation in the post-*Roe* years dealt with such issues as public funding of abortions, limits on services performed in public hospitals with respect to abortions, standards of care with respect to the life of the fetus, viability testing (stage of fetal development), and keeping records of abortions performed.

The political activism and aggressiveness of liberal organizations and their accomplishments during this period were not lost on organizations and their members on the political right. Right-wing forces came to appreciate the growing importance of the Supreme Court in national policymaking. Conservative interests saw the need to petition the courts to counterbalance the perceived tilt toward liberal interests and their claims.

A number of conservative organizations and think tanks (essentially research institutes) emerged during the 1970s in strong opposition to the nation's liberal drift of the previous decade. Such organizations as Americans United for Life Legal Defense Fund (AUL), Eagle Forum, the Heritage Foundation, the Pacific Legal Foundation, and the Washington Legal Foundation exemplified the organizational nature and concerns of this movement.[7]

In the mid-1970s, for example, Americans United for Life Legal Defense Fund assembled a coalition of antiabortion lawyers for purposes of strategy and a sustained attack on *Roe* v. *Wade*. These lawyers were drawn from some of the nation's most prestigious law schools like California–Berkeley and the John Marshall Law School–Chicago. To gain experience and confidence, Americans United for Life Legal Defense Fund began networking with sympathetic attorneys throughout the nation. To supplement this activity, the organization established and disseminated a newsletter, *Lex Vitae,* that contained a summary of pending abortion cases. In addition, to build up its financial coffers, the AUL solicited funds from other pro-life groups promising to support their legislative initiatives and victories. The fund was not successful at first because of the timing of its formation and litigation. Because it utilized litigation to stop the promulgation of adverse legal precedents (e.g., the *Roe* decision), the fund found itself operating in a hostile political climate. But as the political climate began to change in the 1980s, its fund-raising efforts were more successful.

Presently, the organization operates as a "legal backup" for pro-life organizations. It prepares legal briefs and counsels legislative strategies for its allies in Supreme Court presentations. Fund members believe they have made some progress toward their goals, and some of their liberal opponents have voiced similar views. A source from this latter coalition states:

> At the outset, they [the AUL] used tremendously inflammatory rhetoric, out of court and in their briefs, and there was a sad lack of knowledge of federal procedure. But now there's professionalism. Their briefs are smoother; they don't have their hysterical tone to them. Their arguments were nowhere near the exotic kind they've used in other law suits.[8]

Some important differences are apparent between litigating conservative organizations and those of liberal orientation. First, the assumption that only politically disadvantaged groups resort to litigation does not explain the creation of groups to litigate economic issues. Rather, economic litigators do not resort to the courts because they feel disadvantaged in other political forums; rather, they see themselves as judicially disadvantaged. Second, conservative litigators do not cooperate with each other as do liberal organizations. Rather, they prefer to go it alone, and if there is to be cooperation, it is done outside the courtroom.

Thus, we can assume that a wide range of interests regularly resort to litigation because they view the courts as another arena in the struggle for influence. Courtrooms now are viewed no differently from legislative corridors or bureaucratic offices that also serve as arenas for competing interests.

Amicus Curiae Briefs

Amicus curiae (friend of the court) briefs represent a more indirect route to judicial influence. Amicus briefs are interest group inputs to court personnel of additional data and arguments relevant to an impending judicial decision. Samuel Krislov notes:

> Where the stakes are highest for groups, and where needs on the part of judges for information and for sharing responsibility through consultation are at their peak, access [for amicus briefs] has appropriately, and almost inevitably, been [at] its greatest.[9]

Amicus briefs allow more organizations to be heard than merely those party to the suit. Additionally, these briefs inform the courts of the possible or probable consequences of their contents. By demonstrating support or opposition to an impending decision, they can also influence a judge's ruling. Given that many organizations have modest resources with respect to litigation, amicus curiae briefs do provide a broader perspective for judicial decision making.

As the courts, especially the Supreme Court, have broadened their agenda of cases, there has been a corresponding upswing in the submission of amicus briefs. Organizations across the political spectrum from the liberal American Civil Liberties Union to the conservative Washington Legal Foundation utilize the amicus brief as a strategy to gain the attention of the Supreme Court. The high-water mark of submissions is the *Webster* case, which dealt with a challenge to abortion rights by the state of Missouri. In this context, another controversial issue that has come before the high court is the issue of doctor-assisted suicide (or euthanasia). Conflicting interests on both sides of the issue have petitioned the Supreme Court for some kind of definitive decision. The submission of many conflicting amicus curiae briefs is the hallmark of this struggle.

An examination of the issues and organizations involved here along with an analysis of the conflicting amicus briefs can result in a better comprehension of associational argumentation. Each side offers the high court what it believes to be the correct legal basis for a favorable decision. Two cases, Vacco v. Quill, 95-1858, and Washington v. Glucksberg, 96-110, pushed the Supreme Court into the center of the ongoing debate over doctor-assisted suicide. The states of New York and Washington petitioned the high court to ascertain whether their respective laws barring doctor-assisted suicides are constitutional.[10]

Respondent Arguments Favoring Doctor-Assisted Suicide Generally speaking, doctors and physicians challenging the New York and Washington State laws claim that their patients have a Fourteenth Amendment right, under either due process or equal protection, to control the timing and circumstances of their death. Therefore, these doctors claim that laws imposing criminal penalties on those who aid in a person's suicide violate the Constitution. Table 8.1 on pages 126–127 presents the various organizations supporting this position and their respective rationales. A brief examination of the content of a number of these amicus briefs follows.

The Council for Secular Humanism and a majority of these amicus briefs maintain that the right to die is constitutionally protected:

> Compelling a competent person to remain alive under conditions she finds irremediably painful and degrading is starkly inconsistent with

the respect for personal autonomy that is an intrinsic part of our national heritage.[11]

In balancing the interests of the state versus the individual, most of the amicus briefs agree that individual rights outweigh state interests. In their brief, which cited a number of cases, the Americans for Death with Dignity assert:

> The state's interest in preserving life is strongest in the middle point of the continuum after viability and throughout an adult's healthy productive years. As an individual approaches death, the state's interest in the preservation of life weakens.[12]

As noted in Table 8.1, a number of amicus briefs offered equal protection rights under the Fourteenth Amendment. The brief of the American Medical Students Association states:

> There is no clinical basis for distinguishing between patients who can discontinue life support and those who cannot. This statement is contingent upon (1) the intent of the patient or the physician or (2) the extent to which the active intervention of the physician affects the time and manner of the patient's death.[13]

The amicus brief of Surviving Family Members offers experiences to show that the distinction in the laws between withdrawing or refusing life support measures and choosing other forms of physician assistance to hasten the death of a terminally ill patient is meaningless for both patient and family. The amicus brief states:

> In both cases, the patients are facing an inevitable death caused by a fatal disease and are suffering, often unbearably. ... It is not legally sufficient to say that because the state legislatures treat these actions as different, that they are in fact different.[14]

Another legal argument offered by these briefs emanates from Thirty-six Religious Organizations:

> Our long tradition of individual religious liberty and government non-interference with religious decisions, exemplified by the religion clauses of the First Amendment, serves to confirm that the "perplexing question" of physician-assisted suicide with its "unusually strong moral and ethical overtones" (from the Curzon case), is an intimate, personal, and ultimately spiritual decision appropriately reserved to the individual's own conscience ... The many diverse religious faiths represented

TABLE 8.1 Analysis of Amicus Briefs In Support of a Doctor-Assisted Suicide Right

Amicus Briefs Supporting Doctor-Assisted Suicide	Liberty Protection	Equal Protection	No Damage to Medical Profession	States Able to Regulate	Other Arguments
1. National Women's Health Network	X				Threat to women
2. Thirty-six Religious Organizations, separate groups, and individuals	X				First Amendment
3. American Medical Students Association		X	X		
4. Coalition of Bioethics, ad hoc	X		X	X	
5. American Civil Liberties Union and other organizations	X	X	X	X	
6. Coalition of Law Professors, ad hoc		X	X	X	Respect for law

7. Ronald Dworkin and five other philosophers	X			
8. State Legislators, individuals members from sixteen states	X	X		Rule of courts
9. Americans for Death with Dignity	X	X	X	
10. Hospice Professionals			X	
11. Julian Whitaker, physician	X		X	
12. Surviving Family Members	X		X	Anecdotal
13. Gay Men's Health Crisis and others concerned with AIDS, HIV, and those with disabilities	X		X	ADA
14. Center for Reproductive Law	X		X	Women
15. Council for Secular Humanism	X		X	
16. Washington State Psycho-logical Association	X		X	

127

in this country have many diverse views on the theological and moral propriety of physician-assisted suicide.[15]

Argumentation found among the other amicus briefs supporting doctor-assisted suicide demonstrates the breadth and depth of this position. The briefs highlight the complexity of this issue, which involves not only public policy but patient and physician rights.

Petitioners' Amicus Briefs Opposing Doctor-Assisted Suicide The amicus briefs in Table 8.2 on pages 103–132 offer a number of arguments counter to those just noted. Opponents of doctor-assisted suicide hold that it is not constitutionally sanctioned either under due process or the Fourteenth Amendment. Those indulging in the practice of euthanasia must be made subject to various punishments including financial and criminal penalties. Our society's elderly are the most vulnerable, and they must be protected from medical exploitation.

In its brief, the American Hospital Association (AHA) makes a due process argument against doctor-assisted suicide. It bases its position on the previous high court decision in *Bowers* v. *Hardwick,* which states:

> The Court is most vulnerable and comes nearest to illegitimacy when it deals with judge-made constitutional laws having little or no cognizable roots in the language or design of the Constitution ... There should be, therefore, resistance to expand the substantive reach of those Clauses, particularly if it requires redefining the category of rights deemed to be fundamental.[16]

The American Medical Association's brief offers a common argument, namely that "physician-assisted suicide lies outside the continuum of liberty interests that this court has previously recognized as constitutionally protected."

A number of these amicus briefs express concerns regarding the difficulties of regulating such a narrow right. They argue that consent may not be voluntary because patients may be incompetent, may have been coerced, or may not actually be at the end of their life span. The American Geriatric Society's brief argues:

> [T]he competence requirement interacts with the requirement for being terminally ill, since patients tend to lose competence as illness becomes more severe.[17]

Certainly, the amicus briefs of this coalition offer a broader range of legal argumentation than their opponents do. They come from a more varied and broader constituency as well.

The magnitude and the quality of this legal effort (sixty-four amicus briefs) stand second only to the number of briefs submitted in the *Webster* case. These combined briefs represent the collective scholarship of dozens of individual authors. They represent a unique body of countervailing arguments with respect to the issue of life or death.

The Impact of Amicus Briefs With respect to judicial decision making, what degree of influence do submitted amicus briefs have? This, of course, is not easy to discern because little information exists regarding which judges read which briefs. Gregory Calderia and John Wright comment that "some circumstantial evidence suggests that they might very well be important."[18] In their analysis of amicus briefs submitted in the *Webster* case, Lee Epstein and Joseph F. Kobylka note that pro-life organizations used radio programs to send antiabortion messages and information to the high court but also:

> More likely to have some effect were *amicus curiae* briefs, the coordination of which constituted the second focus of [pro-choice and pro-life] movements' strategies. Planned Parenthood ... handled the pro-choice side much as the Association for the Study of Abortion had done in *Roe*. They oversaw the filing of thirty-two separate *amicus curiae* briefs ... It mattered less to them what the briefs said than they showed the broad base of support for *Roe* for mainstream America.[19]

Susan Behuniak-Long analyzed the seventy-eight amicus briefs submitted to the Supreme Court while it was considering the *Webster* case (1989). She states:

> The briefs were not only read; they also had an impact. Their arguments and information helped shape the terms of the Court debate [both during and after oral arguments]. Whether the justices refuted the briefs, modified an argument because of them, or accept and integrated their points, the amici mattered.[20]

Additionally, in their discussion of the amicus briefs in the *Webster* case, Barbara Hinkson Craig and David M. O'Brien state that many of the briefs were aimed at Justice O'Connor because she was considered a pivotal vote. They add that her questioning of the counsels arguing *Webster* indicates that she read a number of the briefs and was "moved" by their arguments.[21]

What impact did these amicus briefs have on the high court's decision concerning doctor-assisted suicide? There is no clear-cut answer. Although the Court ruled unanimously that doctor-assisted suicide is not a constitutional right, the majority opinion was characterized by division. Separate opinions were written by Breyer, O'Connor, Souter, and Stevens. The majority

TABLE 8.2 Analysis of Amicus Briefs in Opposition to a Doctor-Assisted Suicide Right

Amicus Briefs Opposing Doctor-Assisted Suicide	Due Process	Equal Protection	Damage to Medical Profession	Hard to Regulate	Volitional Obstacles	Wrong Role for Courts	Other Arguments
1. Twenty States plus Puerto Rico (Quill)	X	X				X	
2. Bioethics Professors, ad hoc		X					
3. Choice in Dying, Inc.					X	X	
4. New York and Washington State Legislators	X	X					
5. R. Thompson, Prosecutor Oakland County, Mich.	X	X		X			
6. AMA, ANA, APA[a] (Quill)	X	X	X			X	
7. Gary Lee, M.D., care facilities and doctor				X			Protect vulnerable
8. Twenty-one States plus Puerto Rico	X	X		X			Public confidence
9. American Life League		X		X			Criminal
10. Medical Society of N.J.		X	X			X	Stare decisis
11. United States (Quill)	X	X				X	
12. United States (Glucksberg)	X		X			X	
13. U.S. Catholic Conference	X	X					
14. Jerome Decosse, M.D., Metropolitan Catholic Physicians Guild	X	X	X				Source of rights
15. Not Dead Yet		X		X	X		Violates ADA
16. Clarendon Foundation		X					
17. American College of Legal Medicine	X		X		X		Pro-assisted suicide

Organization					Notes
18. Union of Orthodox Jewish Congregations of America	X				
19. Evangelical Lutheran Church of America	X	X			Stress protection
20. National Hospice Organization	X	X	X		Stress hospice
21. National Legal Center for the Medically Dependent and Disabled, Inc.		X			
22. International Anti-Euthanasia Family Living Council	X		X		Managed care
23. Catholic Medical Association	X	X			
24. American Center for Law and Justice	X		X		
25. Catholic Medical Association	X	X	X		
26. Agudath Israel of America (Orthodox Jewish)	X	X	X		Value of life
27. Project on Death in America of Open Society Institute	X		X	X	
28. Rutherford Institute	X			X	
29. Southern Center for Law and Ethics	X		X		Church history
30. E. Michael McCann, D.A., Milwaukee County, Wisconsin		X	X		Criminal
31. American Hospital Association	X	X			
32. Family Research Council	X	X	X		Nazi experience
33. Legal Center Defense of Life, Inc.	X				Inadequate history
34. AMA, ANA, APA[a] (Glucksberg)	X	X			

Continued on page 132

TABLE 8.2 *Continued*

Amicus Briefs Opposing Doctor-Assisted Suicide	Due Process	Equal Protection	Damage to Medical Profession	Hard to Regulate	Volitional Obstacles	Wrong Role for Courts	Other Arguments
35. State of Oregon	X						
36. American Suicide Foundation				X	X	X	Netherlands and depression
37. U.S. Catholic Conference (Glucksberg)	X						
38. National Conference of Persons with Disability	X	X				X	Criminal
39. Senator Hatch and Representatives Hyde and Canady	X					X	
40. National Association of Pro-Life Nurses	X						Nurses' rights
41. Commissioner for Civil Rights		X		X		X	Undermining confidence
42. American Association Homes and Services for the Aging	X	X		X			
43. Christian Legal Society	X	X					Religious discrimination
44. National Spinal Cord Injury Association	X				X		Protection disabled
45. National Right to Life Committee, Inc.	X						
46. Schiller Institute	X						International crimes
47. American Geriatric Society		X	X	X	X		
48. Wayne County, Michigan	X			X	X	X	Political issue

aAmerican Medical Association (AMA), American Nurses Association (ANA), American Psychiatric Association (APA).

opinion (Rehnquist) noted amicus briefs from the state of California and the U.S. government. Justice Breyer's opinion noted amicus briefs from Hospice Professionals and the American Medical Association. Justice Souter's opinion noted the amicus brief jointly submitted by New York and Washington State legislators. Justice Stevens noted the amicus briefs from Bioethics Coalition and from the Washington State Psychological Association. Finally, though it does appear that briefs in support of doctor-assisted suicide were ineffective in this arena, nonetheless, the game may shift to another level or arena where those losers may become winners.

Judicial Selection

Another indirect route for group influence is *judicial selection.* The Supreme Court's expanding agenda noted at the beginning of the chapter is generating increasing organizational concerns with respect to its composition. Past presidents have brought different approaches to the nominating process as well as different philosophies with respect to the high court's decision making.

With respect to the former, President Jimmy Carter (1976–1980) emphasized the use of affirmative action in appointments. More women and minorities were appointed than ever before. For example, Carter appointed 28 blacks out of 206, or 13.6 percent of his district judges; 16 percent of his judges were black and 20 percent of his appellate appointments were women.[22] By contrast, former President Reagan filled only five vacancies with black judges, about 2 percent. Reagan's appointment of women at the district level was about 8 percent and only 10 percent at the appellate level.

The Carter and Reagan selection process also diverged. Carter urged U.S. senators, who usually dominate the selection process, to allow for the establishment of judicial selection panels in their respective states, thereby allowing the panels to screen candidates for nomination. This resulted in depoliticizing the selection process, although most nominees were Democrats. The Reagan administration deemphasized the panels, preferring to rely almost exclusively on senatorial recommendations. In addition, the Reagan administration saw Carter's use of affirmative action as irrelevant and sacrificing "judicial merit" for a political symbolism of a more "representative federal bench." In this context, one source notes:

> The Reagan administration had in place what was probably the most thorough and comprehensive system of recruiting and screening federal judicial candidates of any administration ever. This administration, moreover, attempted to assert the President's prerogatives over judicial selection more consistently than any of its predecessors.[23]

Reasons for this significant change in the judicial appointment process are not hard to find. Like the Democratic coalition it succeeded, the victorious Republican coalition of the 1980s was anchored at one end by lower- to middle-income Northern white ethnics and white Southerners attracted by conservative social policies as enunciated by Reagan and other Republicans (e.g., family values, antiabortion, prayers in schools, a less intrusive federal government, etc.). The other end of the Republican coalition was comprised of an economic and corporate elite who were generously rewarded by tax breaks and other economic policies. In this mix were party evangelical voters who pushed Republican candidates further to the right with their evangelical agenda, mirroring blacks in the Democratic coalition.

During the Reagan years, evangelicals focused on the staffing of the judiciary. Until the judiciary was transformed, these players argued that the attainment of a pro-family, Christian, and moral social agenda would remain largely symbolic. It would not be constitutionally legitimated until a sympathetic judiciary, especially the Supreme Court, was in place. In this context, the White House established the President's Committee on the Federal Judicial Selection, which consisted of key White House staff members and Justice Department personnel. This body screened judicial appointments with an eye on ideological orientation. Extensive interviews were conducted with prospective nominees to the federal bench, and the conservative agenda comprised the basis of the interviews. Such actions as support for the Equal Rights Amendment, being pro-choice on abortion, and contributing to Planned Parenthood or the National Coalition to Ban Handguns were enough to disqualify nominees.

In this context, President Reagan nominated Robert Bork, a federal circuit court judge, to the Supreme Court. Bork had strong academic and conservative credentials. He had written extensively on the Supreme Court and its contemporary role in interpreting the U.S. Constitution. He was the most accomplished, forceful, and unrelenting critic of judicial activism of his generation. The defeat of his nomination, therefore, became a matter of overwhelming importance to moderate and liberal interests.

CASE STUDY:
INTEREST GROUP CONFLICT OVER
THE NOMINATION OF ROBERT BORK

A political battle was virtually assured when Bork was selected, as he would take retiring Lewis Powell's place. Powell was not just a pivotal vote on the Court; in his final two terms, Powell had been the deciding vote over 75 percent of the time.[24] Powell's vote had been key in cases dealing with abortion, affirmative action, and the death penalty. With his departure, the philosophical balance of the Court would shift. Reagan also chose Bork while the Senate was controlled by Democrats, which literally guaranteed that some controversy would occur. Additionally, although Bork had been passed over by earlier Reagan appointments, liberal interest groups made it their business to be acquainted with his record. So when his nomination surfaced, they were well prepared to oppose it.

Immediately after Bork's name was announced for the Powell vacancy, Senator Edward Kennedy denounced Bork, and more than seventy-five other organizations quickly followed suit.[25] The American Civil Liberties Union (ACLU) abandoned its practice of political neutrality and called for Bork's rejection. Only once before had the ACLU taken such a position, and this was in 1971 when it was on record as opposing then-president Nixon's nomination of William Rehnquist to the high court. A sample of interest groups opposing Judge Bork includes:

Alliance for Justice
American Civil Liberties Union
American Federation of State, County, and Municipal Employees
Americans for Religious Liberty
Center for Population Options
Citizen Action
Communications Workers of America
Epilepsy Foundation of America
Federally Employed Women
Federation of Women Lawyers
Friends of the Earth
International Association of Machinists
Mexican-American Women's National Association
National Abortion Rights Action League
National Association of Social Workers
National Coalition to Abolish the Death Penalty
National Conference of Women's Bar Association
National Council of La Raza
National Gay and Lesbian Task Force
National Lawyer's Guild
National Urban League
National Women's Health Network
9 to 5, National Association of Working Women
People for the American Way
Rainbow Lobby
Sane/Freeze
Sierra Club
United States Student Association
YWCA/USA

Promising a "no holds barred battle," the AFL-CIO came out in opposition, which is something it had not done since joining with others to defeat Nixon's nominations of Judges Haynesworth and Carswell.[26]

These groups quickly set up task forces in opposition to Bork.[27] A *lobbying task force* of about two dozen organizations was established to contact senators and ask them not to take a position until the hearings took place. The idea was to "freeze the Senate." This task force also began to identify senators who would comprise their primary and secondary targets. A *grass-roots task force* was established for three stages of action: a prehearing phase, a hearing phase, and the floor phase. The purpose of the prehearing phase was to alert as many opponent organizations as possible throughout the country. These, in turn, were urged to help shape public sentiment against Bork through rallies, dissemination of literature, letters to the editor, and ads in state and local newspapers. Objectives of the hearing and floor phases were to initiate a larger public grass-roots movement and institute a letter-writing campaign through social clubs, churches and labor unions.

A *media task force* was orchestrated and led by such organizations as People for the American Way (PAW), NARAL, Planned Parenthood, and the American Federation of State, County, and Municipal Employees (AFSCME). These organizations spent over $1 million in the late summer and early fall of 1987 on radio, television, and print messages. The idea was to alert the public with respect to the crucial role the Senate would play with respect to the roles of advise and consent on presidential appointees.

A *drafting task force* began work in late summer to identify and develop themes and messages for the lobbying campaign. Its purposes were to develop themes that would be relatively simple and straightforward but compelling enough to galvanize citizen action groups. Important here was to find themes that would appeal to diverse interests within the anti-Bork coalition. The National Women's Law Center played a key role in supplying an extensive analysis of Judge Bork's opinions and writings.

Prior to the hearings, the anti-Bork message was finalized that contained three themes: (a) Bork was not a fair-minded person, (b) he was generally insensitive to civil rights and equal justice for women and minorities, and (c) he was an extremist judge who was out of the mainstream. These themes were quickly transmitted through the grass-roots communication system to senators and members of the lobbying task force. They also found their way into newsprint and radio ads across the country. Through their forum, People for the American Way stated:

> Bork's own writings and speeches indicate he would vote to turn back the clock of progress, retrenching on civil rights gains made in our last four decades, undermining the constitutional right to privacy, and restricting free speech clearly protected from such restrictions in the First Amendment of the Bill of Rights.[28]

Conservative and pro-Bork organizations were galvanized into action to counter their opponents' charges. A sampling of these organizations includes:

Ad Hoc Committee in Defense of Life
American Conservative Union
American Farm Bureau Federation
American Legislative Exchange Council
Americans for Tax Reform
Center for Judicial Studies
Christian Action Council
Christian Voice
Coalitions for America
College Republican Nation Committee
Concerned Women for America
Conservative Leadership PAC
Council for National Policy, Inc. (CNP, Inc.)
Federal Criminal Investigators' Association
Fraternal Order of Police
Free the Court
International Association of Chiefs of Police
Moral Majority
National District Attorney's Association
National Jewish Coalition
National Republican Heritage Group's Council
National Sheriff's Association
National Trooper's Association
Renaissance Women
Victims Assistance Legal Organization
We the People

The leaders of such organizations as the American Conservative Union, Concerned Women of America, and the Fraternal Order of Police took the lead in setting up a counteractive lobbying campaign and targeting a dozen or so conservative senators. These individuals were being lobbied extensively by the anti-Bork vote on the floor of the Senate. In this context, the National Right to Life Committee's newspaper, *Right to Life News*, editorialized:

It is our job as citizens who have followed the nomination carefully to contact our Senators to make two points. First, that Bork is extraordinarily competent with a richly varied background in the law, and a razor sharp mind. Second, they oughtn't knuckle under to such extremist special interests as NOW, NARAL, and Planned Parenthood.[29]

At the same time pro-Bork forces were gearing up for Senate hearings, the White House adopted the strategy of recasting Bork's conservative image so as to make the opposition appear more shrill and uncompromising. In this context, presidential aides prepared a 70-page briefing book that was soon followed by a 240-page report from the Justice Department portraying Bork as a "mainstream jurist." These documents were disseminated to Republican senators.[30]

The Hearings

The Bork confirmation hearings were unprecedented in the number of pro and con witnesses and organizations testifying (120), the length Bork's testimony before the Senate Judiciary Committee (4.5 days), the supporting testimony of former high-level Republicans on behalf of Bork (former President Gerald Ford and former Chief Justice Warren Burger), and White House pressure on Republican members of the committee. In addition, the staff of the democratically controlled committee issued its own 72-page study refuting the administration's "centrist" depiction of Bork.[31] A letter from former President Jimmy Carter opposing Bork's confirmation was also read into the record.

During his long testimony before the senators, Bork tried to give the appearance of a moderate or even a centrist jurist. Besides trying to desert much of his past record, Bork went to great length to assure committee members as to how he might vote if confirmed. By the time he finished testifying, Bork contradicted much of what he originally stood for and for which he had been nominated. Noting this considerable difference, Senator Arlen Specter stated, "I think what many of us are looking for is where you are."[32]

Chairman Joe Biden presided over the hearings in a measured, meticulously fair manner that won praise from Republican Senators Orrin Hatch, Alan Simpson, and Strom Thurmond. Biden was also advised by conservative law professor Philip Kurland to frame the debate broadly in terms of the high court's role in protecting individual rights (e.g., the right to privacy) rather than focusing on narrower and more divisive issues (e.g., affirmative action and abortion). The debate was more about the meaning of the Constitution than about Robert Bork.

The fundamental issue raised by the hearings, then, was the view of the Constitution shared by Bork and the Reagan administration. According to one source,

> The American Bar Association's Committee on Federal Judiciary split over Bork's qualifications to sit on the high court and approximately 2000 law professors across the nation wrote letters opposing Bork's nomination.[33]

The Confirmation Decision

Organizations on both sides of the confirmation battle instituted grass-roots campaigns to generate further pressure on Senate members. Phyllis Schlafly, president of Eagle Forum, a leading pro-family organization, urged the members of her organization to contact their senators and say, "Please confirm Robert Bork of the Court." In addition, Bork's Senate supporters were able to delay the voting to give their forces more opportunities to target selected senators with letters, telegrams, and phone calls.

The national publicity plus pressure group tactics whip-sawed the members of the judiciary committee. Just days prior to the committee's vote, seven Southern senators led by Louisiana's Bennette Johnston announced their opposition. This along with similar pronouncements by Republican Senator Arlen Specter and Democrat Dennis DeConcini prodded the two remaining Democrats on the committee, Robert Byrd and Howell Heflin, to join their ranks. Thus, the committee voted nine to five not to recommend Bork for the Court vacancy. Shortly thereafter, the full Senate voted fifty-eight to forty-two also to reject Bork. By the widest margin ever, Robert Bork became the twenty-seventh nominee to be rejected by the Senate.

Interests opposed to Bork's nomination were successful because they offered simple and compelling messages to both the voting senators and the general public. Bork's supporters offered more diffuse arguments such as the "radical left versus America" and the left's "raw politics" in opposition. Bork's opponents were more effective in getting their message out and utilized the mass media to reach a broader audience. The political base of anti-Bork players was also broader (about 300 organizations against to approximately 100 in favor). More important, the former included more moderate and middle-of-the-road organizations like the National Council of Churches, the National Federation of Business and Professional Women's Club, and Service Station Dealers of America. Finally, many senators found Bork's views of the Constitution too extreme.

GROUP COMPLIANCE/NONCOMPLIANCE WITH SUPREME COURT DECISIONS

Once a case has been argued before the Supreme Court and it hands down its decision, the litigants are expected to comply. The high court has no enforcement mechanism of its own. Thus, compliance depends in part on how those affected by the decision accept or do not accept it. Supreme Court decisions frequently affect a broad range of citizens and organizations such as environmentalists, women, racial minorities, colleges and universities, and so on. A whole range of established procedures, informal practices, and behavioral patterns can be disturbed in the wake of a high court decision.

Our federal system with its inherent decentralization of power allows a broad range of responses to judicial decisions. Some interests may seek to evade the responsibilities assigned to them by the decision. There can also be conflicting interpretations of a decision, or a decision may be seen as ambiguous. Responses, for example, by conservative political interests and state and local officials, though generally hostile to the Supreme Court's 1954 *Brown* decision, displayed a good deal of variation. The Virginia legislature initiated a new body of laws aimed at frustrating compliance. North and South Carolina adopted pupil placement programs. Further, some states allowed for the leasing of public school facilities to private organizations, which then operated them on a segregated basis. Civil rights organizations appealed to federal courts again, and most of these strategies were overturned by federal circuit courts.

Legislative compliance came a lot quicker with respect to the Warren Court's rulings with respect to legislative reapportionment. In *Baker* v. *Carr* (1962),[34] the high court ruled that the Tennessee house was apportioned in such a way that it discriminated against growing urban areas like Shelby County, which contains the city of Memphis. Under growing pressure from urban voters, the rules of the game were changed, and the Tennessee house was reapportioned during the next legislative session. Two years later (1964), Warren applied the same principle to congressional districts in *Wesberry* v. *Sanders* (Georgia).[35] Subsequently, urban players in other states successfully petitioned the high court for a significant change in legislative reapportionment procedures.

As the activist Warren Court handed down further precedent-setting decisions, criticisms among conservative political players began to emerge—the John Birch Society, the Heritage Foundation, and Americans for Constitutional Action—strongly condemning both the decisions and the high court for its activist role. These interests saw the court moving into areas that historically were within the province of the states. Within a relatively short span of 6 years, general compliance to the principle of equal representation (i.e., "one person, one vote") was attained.

A far different picture emerges if one looks at interest compliance with respect to prayer in public schools. Through a series of decisions over the past 25 years, the Supreme Court has almost unanimously rejected religious exercises in the public schools (e.g., bible reading, recitation of prayers, moments of silence, etc.).[36] But many public officials and ad hoc religious organizations have continued these practices. An alliance of the Christian coalition Eagle Forum and other conservative players are pushing for a constitutional amendment that would overturn earlier Court decisions banning prayer in classrooms.

As one can see, compliance or noncompliance reveals a spectrum of differing responses. Behavior depends on the perceived threat or effect of a court decision. Our decentralized political system allows concerned interests a good deal of latitude in deciding what course of action is best for them.

As the previous pages illustrate, different combinations of organized interests perceive the federal judiciary as an important forum of policymaking. Various coalitions utilize a number of different strategies to affect the policy outcomes of this branch. Lobbying this branch, however, requires approaches different from the other two branches. Judges must demonstrate greater isolation and greater objectivity in responding to group claims.

Today, the Supreme Court in particular is deciding what constitutes a "religious" exercise in the public schools, when a woman may have an abortion, or what the composition is of a congressional district. This expansionist role of the nation's highest court will undoubtedly continue well beyond the year 2000.

Finally, the courts must look to others for implementation of their decisions. This means that public and private citizens at all levels of government and private sectors can become involved (e.g., a corporation CEO, a governor, a university or college president, or some public agency). Acceptance of a judicial decision may occur very quickly, or a combination of organizations or individuals in opposition may delay it or modify its ultimate impact.

NOTES

1. Alex de Tocqueville, *Democracy in America* (New York: Mentor Books, 1965), p. 75.
2. Felix Frankfurter, "The Supreme Court and the Public," *Forum* 83 (1930), p. 332.
3. Nathan Glazer, "The Imperial Presidency," *Public Interest* 95 (1985), p. 106.
4. Marc K. Landy, Marc J. Roberts, and Stephen R. Thomas, *The Environmental Protection Agency: Asking the Wrong Questions from Nixon to Clinton* (New York: Oxford University Press, 1994), especially Chapter 2.
5. Richard Cortner, "Strategies and Tactics of Litigants of Constitutional Cases," *Journal of Public Law* 17 (1986), p. 287.
6. Lee Epstein and Joseph F. Kobylka, *The Supreme Court and Legal Change* (Chapel Hill: University Press of North Carolina Press, 1992), pp. 160–165.
7. Lee Epstein, *Conservatives in Court* (Knoxville: University of Tennessee Press, 1985), pp. 95–104.
8. Ibid., p. 116.
9. Samuel Krislov, "The Amicus Curiae Brief: From Friendship to Advocacy," *Yale Law Review* 72 (1963), pp. 703–704.

10. A good deal of the following material comes from "Bifocal," *American Bar Association* 17 (1997), pp. 1-8.
11. Amicus Brief, Council for Secular Humanism, p. 2.
12. Amicus Brief, Americans for Death with Dignity, pp. 8–9.
13. Amicus Brief, American Medical Students, p. 2.
14. Amicus Brief, Surviving Family Members, pp. 27–29.
15. Amicus Brief, Thirty-six Religious Organizations, p. 2.
16. Bowers v. Hardwick, 478 U.S. 186 (1986), 194–195.
17. "Bifocal," op. cit., p. 2.
18. Gregory A. Calderia and John R. Wright, "Amici Curiae before the Supreme Court: Who Participates, When, and How Much," *Journal of Politics* 52 (1990), p. 788.
19. Lee Epstein and Joseph F. Kobylka, op. cit., pp. 269, 272.
20. Quoted in Barbara H. Craig and David M. O'Brien, *Abortion and American Politics* (Chatham, NJ: Chatham House, 1993), pp. 224, 226.
21. Ibid., p. 227.
22. David M. O'Brien, "The Reagan Judges: His Most Enduring Legacy?" in *The Reagan Legacy: Promise and Performance,* Charles O. Jones, ed. (Chatham, NJ: Chatham House, 1988) p. 66.
23. Stephen Markham, "Memorandum for Attorney General Meese: A Comparison of Judicial Selection Procedures" and quoted by O'Brien, Ibid., p. 67.
24. Interview with Justice Lewis Powell in the *Los Angeles Times,* May 3, 1987, p. 1.
25. Some of these were the Alliance for Justice, the National Association for the Advancement of Colored People (NAACP), and the National Abortion Rights Action League (NARAL).
26. *AFL-CIO News,* April 29, 1987.
27. See John R. Wright, *Interest Groups and Congress* (Boston: Allyn and Bacon, 1996), pp. 97–99.
28. "Tell Your Senator to Oppose Bork," *People for the American Way Newsletter,* October 15, 1987.
29. "Have You Contacted Your US Senators About the Confirmation of Judge Bork?" *Right to Life News,* October 15, 1987.
30. *Cardozo Law Review* 9 (1987), pp. 187–200.
31. O'Brien, op. cit., p. 91.
32. Ibid., p. 92.
33. Ibid., p. 93.
34. 369 U.S. 1.
35. 376 U.S. 1.
36. The most authoritative decision by the Supreme Court with respect to the "separation of church and state" today is Lemon v. Kurtzman, 403 U.S. 602 (1971).

9

Summary and Conclusions

The Shape of Interest Group Politics Beyond 2000

INTRODUCTION

As we have seen, the battle for political influence is continuous. Many interests are involved in different arenas and across different time frames. A presidential budget (e.g., submission and enactment) involves a fairly specific time frame, whereas congressional formulation of a farm bill can take months or years to finalize. In addition, different policy initiatives bring forth differing combinations of groups. Foreign policymaking usually involves the White House, whereas a rural irrigation project is of more concern to congressional personnel and local organizations. Just about everything government does involves winning and losing. Nonetheless, even struggling interests (e.g., veterans, women, or unionists) remain active to increase their chances of winning next time or next year.

PARTICIPANTS IN THE POWER GAME

For purposes of review, we need to recount some of the key people in the influence or power game. They do not represent a cross section of the nation. Because of differing motivations and skills, today's interest group universe disproportionately overrepresents the better educated, higher income, and better informed sectors of society. In simple terms, the "haves" play the influence game better than the "have nots." Governmental policymaking has traditionally catered to the concerns of the former and not the latter.

Consequently, business and professional associations and other profit-oriented interests have been consistent winners in the American political system. The latter's organizational skills, such as leadership, communication, and information gathering, contribute to a dominant and continuing role in national policymaking. These interests, though, should not be thought of as a monolithic bloc; they do indulge in fractious struggles over such issues as international trade, governmental regulation, and/or domestic monetary policies.

We must also appreciate the fact that the battle for influence is *inclusive*, not *exclusive*. From time to time, new combinations of interests become participants. Such was the case of environmental interests in the late 1960s and early 1970s. The decades of the 1980s and 1990s have witnessed another influx of players such as Hispanics, Asians, antiabortionists, religious fundamentalists, and the homeless. Each is seeking some policy goal: better housing, the teaching of family values in schools, or the extension of civil rights. There is no reason to doubt that beyond the year 2000 a new set of players with specific goals will enter the fray.

Of course, there are also cyclic patterns of influence or political power evident among participants. Some may be initially successful after formalization (e.g., pro-choice organizations in the 1970s and early 1980s). But with the rise of counterforces, winners may be displaced by others. In this context, inherent organizational characteristics are important as well. These include such factors as internal cohesion, maintenance, affluence, and public perception.

Political parties are also important. It is incorrect to dismiss the parties in spite of the frequent comment that "the party's over." We have already seen that there is a good deal of overlap between various activities of political interest groups and political parties. We know, for example, that parties encompass certain constituencies. Republicans generally have business and politically conservative interests, whereas Democrats receive a great deal of support from working-class and liberal organizations. Despite E. E. Schattschneider's somewhat critical view of organized interests, the past quarter century has seen growing cooperation (thought some might argue displacement) between interest groups and political parties. Recalling previous discussions of political action committees (PACs), increasing monetary support has been gained by party candidates that was not available before. In the long run, only time will tell whether this is a healthy or debilitating development.

This linkage also entails the party-in-government dimension. Given the fact that both the legislative and executive branches of government operate along partisan lines, interest group access to party-in-government officials is vital. With respect to legislative policymaking, access to various chamber leaders, committee chairpeople, and senior personnel is necessary to impact legislative content. Rapport must not only be maintained with a host of congressional personnel in these efforts, but lobbying forces must also appreciate the unique rules of procedure of the Congress as opposed to those of the executive branch or bureaucracy. The convergence of legislative parties and interest groups can be transitory. A successful combination of the two may be replaced by another next week or next month.

Partisanship plays differently across the executive branch. Many top policymakers are appointed, as well as others further down the policymaking ladder. Democratic presidents and other national Democrats seek to appoint to high posts those supporting their policies. Republican presidents and their allies seek to do the same when they control the White House. This aspect of the policy battle involves pressures and demands by respective party constituencies to influence nominations. Business interests, along with those of farmers, veterans, women, and so forth, petition the White House and their party leaders in Congress for support. Given the power bases of both the legislative and executive arenas, parties and interest groups combine their efforts to choose the most supportive.

Though not discussed at length earlier, issue networks are also important participants. In many policy realms, interest groups, administrative personnel, legislators, and others with certain policy expertise are brought together. Retirees, physicians, or representatives for the elderly interact for purposes of influence with committee or subcommittee personnel drafting and administering welfare legislation. Each side needs the other. Bureaucrats need support from interests in interpreting the new law, and legislators need interest group support in passing the legislation as well as future campaign help. These same interests may face off several times a year in relatively confidential meetings. More recently, because of such broader issues as civil rights, military policy, and environmental issues, these networks have come to include more participants now, and their deliberations are more public as well.

Further, state and local interests participate in the policy struggle. Organizations like the National Governor's Association, the National Conference of State Legislators, and the Conference of Mayors frequently interact with various Washington officials with respect to such issues as public housing, urban renewal, infrastructure repair, and so on. Our system of federalism virtually requires that advocates in one institutional arena (state or local) work with advocates in other arenas (national). The point is that policymaking in one area can have serious implications for activists in other areas.

Finally, grass-roots organizations are important. For instance, Mothers Against Drunk Drivers (MADD) gained a good deal of public visibility and political influence during the 1980s. This organization, founded by mothers of children who were killed by drunk drivers, raised an important national issue of raising the legal drinking age of drivers on the nation's streets and highways. In 1983, then-Secretary of Transportation Elizabeth Dole and senators from both parties publicly announced their support for national legislation setting a uniform drinking age.* Although this effort was not successful, Dole and her senatorial supporters succeeded in passing legislation using federal highway funds as an incentive to the states to establish a uniform drinking age.

Many interests exist and are active on this level. Examples are senior citizens, church organizations, developers, liquor and beer distributors, unionists, and neighborhood associations. Important, as well as lobbying targets, are mayor and city council personnel because of their policymaking positions. Activism among local organizations frequently concerns such issues as crime and violence, property taxes, local school curriculum, decaying neighborhoods, and heavy traffic flow. Occasionally, a local organization (e.g., a neighborhood or civil rights organization) resorts to marches and demonstrations as a way of intensifying pressure on local policymakers.** Most of the time, however, local organizations follow the more traditional approaches of lobbying on behalf of, or going public with respect to, their grievances.

STRATEGIES

To win a competition, a plan or set of strategies is necessary. Effective political strategies can differentiate winners from losers. As shown, differing policy arenas and differing combinations of groups require a wide set of strategies. What works with the Congress does not necessarily work with administrative forums. Furthermore, a successful White House strategy may not be acceptable before the nation's highest court. With this in mind, a few strategies can be identified.

Bargaining and Compromise

Bargaining and compromise are important for political success. Remember that these processes come down to us from the nation's founding and are as important now as they were then. The point is that a group coalition maximizes its strength instead of playing a lone game. A combination of inter-

---

*Soon after MADD was established, an intensive lobbying campaign started at the state level which did raise the legal age for drinking. Between the late 1970s and 1983, some nineteen states raised their legal drinking age to 19.

**The Association of Community Organizations for Reform Now (ACORN) has indulged in these types of activities in the past.

ests can be successful by stressing the importance of attaining the ultimate goal and its benefits. This reduces interorganizational tensions and infighting to a degree. Compromise in this context means participants show flexibility with respect to goal attainment. A combination of environmentalists or women accepts some accommodation to their opposition when Congress enacts relevant legislation. The old adage "half a loaf is better than no loaf" comes to mind. In other circumstances, one combination of interests supports another combination in what is called "logrolling" (e.g., throwing one's support behind a general appropriations bill in which a range of players receives some kind of monetary benefit).

Inclusive Effort

Supporting an inclusive effort is another winning strategy. Though some antipluralists argue (see Chapter 2) that existing interests prefer to keep newcomers out, numbers are important in a democracy. It makes sense to believe in the importance of maintaining the status quo. By excluding others, dominant interests impact the rules and acquire more benefits for themselves. Organized labor for a time in the twentieth century was indifferent to civil rights organizations. But with the coming civil rights movement in the late 1950s and 1960s, labor unions reluctantly opened their ranks to more minority workers. Over time, local unions and civil rights groups cooperated in attaining each other's goals, and they continue to work together for both union as well as minority rights. We have also seen how the influx of environmental organizations has changed the parameters of competition.

Organizational Permanence or Persistence

One other strategy for victory is organizational permanence or persistence. Because politics are ongoing, only organizations that persist phase after phase have opportunities to be successful. Of course, some may participate only temporarily and then drop out, such as in the late 1970s and early 1980s when the American Agriculture Movement emerged, flowered, and then withered.[1] But rarely are some issues solved once and for all; abortion rights are still contentious today despite the Supreme Court's ruling in *Roe v. Wade*. Affirmative action, growing out of the 1964 Civil Rights Act, is under fire across the states today as well. The point is, as with these examples, that a victory is rarely complete, and winners must be constantly vigilant. Pro-choice forces are continuously fighting attempts by states to limit the application of abortion rights. Victories are not the end but rather a new beginning. Losers look for strategies and actions that will redeem their causes and overturn their opponents' victories (like the antiaffirmative action activists lobbying for its cancellation). Individuals and organizations cannot hope to win unless they constantly monitor ongoing developments.

CHANGING THE RULES

The U.S. Constitution is generally accepted as America' basic set of legal rules. But laws and procedures of various institutions are also important in determining political influence. Procedures, such as bill referral, House committee/subcommittee procedures, and customs affect the outcomes of political decisions.

But rules are not immutable. What was unconstitutional yesterday may be constitutional today. Our basic law is subject to constant reinterpretation because of changing social attitudes, changing technologies, and evolving socioeconomic conditions. In this context, the issue of abortion rights comes to mind. The Supreme Court's decision in *Roe* v. *Wade* struck down a host of state laws banning abortion and changed the status quo as far as privacy rights were concerned. This decision not only catalyzed organizations on both sides of the issue but also forced rules changes across the states with respect to personal privacy.

Technological advances are also affecting the nation's political agenda. Scientific advances in organ transplants, genetic engineering, and laser surgery are cases in point. Public policymakers now have to come up with a new set of rules to determine who will benefit from these advances and who will not. Additionally, the increasing uses of computers, electronic mail, and cellular phones challenge national policymakers with respect to how this technology can be used and under what circumstances. These decisions have important consequences for individual privacy.

STRATEGIES FOR RULES CHANGES

Proponents of rules changes have a number of strategies to choose from. A constitutional amendment is a viable option. The battle over the Equal Rights Amendment (ERA) in the 1970s is an example. This struggle to change the rules with respect to sex discrimination pitted coalitions of national organizations against each other. Ratification of the ERA, strongly pushed by liberal activist women's organizations and other players, was concerned with nullifying various aspects of claimed sex discrimination (e.g., in job opportunities, rates of pay, and sexual harassment) emanating from statutory, administrative, and constitutional law.

Anti-ERA forces, comprised essentially of conservative women's organizations, strongly opposed the amendment. These groups maintained that the ERA would disrupt family life in America, make women subject to the military draft, and contribute to a higher divorce rate.

State legislatures were the forums where this battle was played out. Ultimately, anti-ERA forces prevailed, as the amendment did not attain the ratification of the required thirty-eight states. Despite their relatively greater resources and public visibility, amendment supporters were not able to convince many state legislators (especially those in Southern and Rocky Mountain states) of their arguments.[2]

Declining confidence in government and increasing public distrust of politicians have fueled a national grass roots movement to limit the terms of public officials, notably members of Congress and state officials. At the present time, such proposals are quite popular across the political spectrum. More than twenty states have enacted legislation, but the Congress has not followed suit.

Proponents of term limits argue that they are needed to keep new blood flowing into government. More specifically, members of Congress who are constantly reelected become career politicians and develop an "inside the Beltway mentality" (in reference to the circle of interstate highways that surrounds Washington). Further, senior members of Congress frequently respond more to special interests than to their constituents.

Opponents of term limits argue that they infringe on voters' freedom of choice. If voters are upset with their representative, they should use the ballot to "throw the rascal out." Opponents further argue that a constant turnover in legislative personnel makes inexperienced legislators much more vulnerable to lobbyists and other careerists in the administrative agencies. Term limits would weaken the overall institution of Congress, leaving it less capable of checking the power of large, well-established lobbies.

This attempt at rules change is now in the judicial arena. In 1995, the Supreme Court ruled that states cannot limit the terms of their congressional representatives:

Such a state-imposed restriction is contrary to the "fundamental principle of our representative democracy," embodied in the Constitution that "the people should choose whom they please to govern them" *Powell* v *McCormack* (1969). Allowing individual states to adopt their own qualifications for Congressional service would be inconsistent with the framers' vision of a uniform national legislature representing the people of the United States. If the qualifications set forth in the text of the Constitution are to be changed, the text must be amended.[3]

Therefore, any rules changes with respect to congressional term limits require either a constitutional amendment or a change in Supreme Court decisions.

Earlier pages alluded to the controversy with respect to campaign finance. Various associations on both the right and the left agree that abuses in the present system require some kind of rules change. But most want changes that do not hamper their ability to raise funds or spend them in ways that enhance their political access or influence. Some organizations, like businesses, want new rules changes restricting labor union contributions. Similarly, labor unions want restrictions on corporate giving. The issue is currently being played out in the legislative arena. One must keep in mind that the old rules work pretty well for 535 members of Congress. There is little incentive for changing them. Winning reelection is a strong motive in the lives of legislators. Therefore, what kind of rules changes, if any, will come about remains an open question.

CONCLUSIONS

What will be the nature of politics and its participants in the year 2000 and beyond? One must be careful in predicting the political future and/or anticipating significant rules changes. Recalling the 1970s, for example, a rule change intended to protect labor unions led to the proliferation of PACs. Similarly, efforts to limit costs of campaigning often served to protect incumbents. But the consequences of doing nothing are also unacceptable. Although the interest group universe is an evolving phenomenon, several assumptions can be made with respect to its future characteristics.

1. Washington will continue to be the focus of interest group formation and activism. The "K Street Corridor" (a prestigious downtown corridor of glass and marble buildings housing hundreds of lobbyists and lobbying firms) will continue to experience growth and diversification. More firms and organizations realize the need for some kind of Washington presence in order to be heard and be politically effective. The corridor is presently comprised of a veritable "who's who" with respect to lobbies and lobbyists (e.g., Bethlehem Steel and USX, Boeing Aircraft, American Council of Life Insurance, Society of American Foresters, Wine and Spirits Wholesalers of America, etc.). This pattern of growth will continue well beyond the year 2000.

2. Improvements in modern technologies and communication will further enhance lobbying opportunities. Lobbyists and their firms have an array of technological systems that generate a good deal of timely political information. Fax machines, satellite television, and computers are the search engines of both today and tomorrow. National television networks and newspapers today have extensive Web pages. Electronic means allow lobbyists to search quite quickly and easily for information on Capitol Hill or about some agency. One can expect that there will be further refinements and improvements in electronic media.

3. Continuing expansion of the national government into more and more areas of governmental activity ensures the continuing growth of a new generation of interest groups. As one source puts it:

[T]he importance of [interest] groups very often lies not in their greatly exaggerated ability to create or to advocate successfully new brand politics, but rather in the ability of policies to generate new interest groups. And, once established, a group will inevitably work to sustain the policy that gave it life. If policy is primarily "created" by Congress, to interest groups—the "offspring" of policy—accrues its care and feeding.[4]

As the national government continues to traverse further into new policy areas, it provides an impetus for the establishment of new organizations such as support groups for AIDS patients or advocacy groups for the homeless. Once securely rooted in Washington, these organizations focus their energies on protecting their turf and advancing the interests of their clients. Moreover, the inability of national policymakers to gain firm administrative control over all of the programs they institute allows interest groups to become integral actors in the implementation process. In short, as the national government expands, it not only mobilizes more interests but enlarges the scope of group politics.

4. The continuing decline in influence and public support for political parties strengthens interest group influence for future activities. Allan Cigler and Burdett Loomis note:

The weakness of political parties has helped created a vacuum in electoral politics since 1960, and in recent years interest groups have moved aggressively to fill it.[5]

Over the past quarter century, many interest groups have adopted techniques of influence traditionally employed by the major parties. For instance, many have aggressively moved into the areas of constituent education and voter mobilization, long the province of parties, whereas most groups prior to 1960 engaged in institutional lobbying (e.g., committee chairs and agency bureaucrats) by exchanging technical advice and information and on occasion by applying pressure. These contacts, however, did not include political donations, nor did they usually include contact or exchanges with constituents. As already seen, various interests not only allocate large sums to political campaigns but also organize grass-roots campaigns and disseminate campaign literature.

In this context, there has been a coalescing of group–party efforts in recent years with various business associations coordinating their electoral contributions with the Republican National Committee. The ability of today's interest groups to become more prominent and involved in political party strategies is an indication of both the weakness of parties and the growing influence of interest groups.

5. Although business organizations remain the dominant type of interest represented in Washington, they are being actively challenged by a number of public interest groups including consumer, environmental, and welfare groups. Much of the twentieth century has witnessed the political dominance of interests representing manufacturing, industry, and finance. The battle for influence played out nationally among these interests ranged from tariff policy to tax and antitrust legislation. As precursors to a new generation of players, these interests were able to "capitalize on their economic leverage and fragmentation of power in the constitutional system itself to establish a firm political presence in national policy."[6]

The past quarter century, however, has witnessed a new set of participants entering the struggle for influence. These are upper-middle-class professionals and intellectuals who have been shaped by their civil rights and antiwar (Vietnam) experiences. These coalitions and certain entrepreneurs (Ralph Nader) established a range of "public interest" organizations (already noted in Chapter 3). Distinguishing themselves from other interests—especially business—they seek to promote the general welfare of all citizens and not just their members. Various elements among public interest organizations (e.g., consumers and environmentalists) have won political victories over big business and big labor by successfully lobbying Congress for restrictions on the manner in which goods are produced, on capital investment, and on the flow of federal resources to established economic interests.

Some 200 years ago, the Founding Fathers prescribed what they believed would be a cure for the ills of interest group politics or "factions." Let them flourish, Madison reasoned, because the more they flourished, the more arduous would be the task of one faction imposing its will on all the others. But as we have seen, the ranks of interest groups have swelled far beyond what the Founders could have anticipated. Today, political interest groups are more numerous, better entrenched, and better equipped to influence national policymaking than ever before.

Conventional wisdom argues that the political pressure exerted by so many organizations has led to the expansion of governmental activities and services. Yet research cited earlier notes that the expansionist mode of Washington has been aided by congressional and administrative entrepreneurs. As Washington continued to traverse into new policy frontiers, it also tended to stimulate political interest and activities among groups previously established for nonpolitical purposes.

In addition, many scholars contend that interest groups and the political game have undergone a metamorphosis over the past quarter century. They have done so either out of choice or necessity by adopting various methods traditionally the purview of the major political parties. The upshot of this process has been a blurring of the distinctions between interest group and party politics and changes in the political status of both. There is also little reason to doubt that the functions of both will intersect even further in the future.

Ironically, Madison and others hoped that a strong central government would be a bulwark against a combination of factions that would emerge within the nation. They would be quite surprised today to find government not only encouraging interest group formation but also accommodating these conflicting interests through a series of arenas, formal and informal procedures, and bargaining. Government policies, then, emanate from ongoing competition among diverse combinations of citizen organizations. This situation is not ideal, but democracy is not given to awarding fair and equitable treatment to all citizens in all political disputes.

NOTES

1. See Allan Cigler and Burdett Loomis, *Interest Group Politics*, 3rd ed. (Washington, DC: CQ Press, 1991), pp. 81–108.
2. See H. R. Mahood, *Interest Group Politics in America: A New Intensity* (Upper Saddle River, NJ: Prentice Hall, 1990), pp. 34–37.
3. Quote from *U.S. Term Limits* v. *Thornton*, 114 S. Ct. 2703 (1995).
4. Ann M. Martino and Cynthia Cates Colella, contributions, "The Transformation in American Politics: Implications for Federalism" (Commission Report) (Washington, DC: Advisory Commission on Intergovernmental Relations, 1986), p. 230.
5. Cigler and Loomis, op. cit., p. 20.
6. Walter Dean Burnham, *Democracy in the Making* (Upper Saddle River, NJ: Prentice Hall, 1983), p. 206.

Key Terms

Access A granted or privileged position of contact where one is listened to by officials in various decision making arenas.

Adjudication A quasi-judicial process of rule making that has important policy consequences for various interest groups.

Administrative rules Guidelines and procedures established by various executive agencies to implement congressional legislation.

Amicus curiae briefs "Friend of the court" briefs submitted by an outside party offering a series of "pro" and "con" arguments on a case before the court.

Clients (Clientele) Individuals or groups with interests closely allied with some agency for the purpose of gaining certain benefits.

Coalition A temporary grouping of individuals or groups supporting a particular policy position.

Collective benefits Certain goods and services (e.g., clean air, water) available to all citizens and not those of a certain group.

Connections Knowing the right persons in the political process and having access to them that possibly results in favorable decisions.

Constituents Individuals to whom elected officials are responsible and from whom they receive support.

Delegated legislation Legislation passed by the Congress allowing a degree of flexibility in policy direction as far as a federal agency is concerned.

Distributive policy A policy that grants benefits to a broad segment of the population as opposed to a few beneficiaries.

Elitism A theory holding that key political decisions are made by a relatively small number of socioeconomically advantaged individuals.

Feedback Information concerning the implementation of policies flowing back to various policymakers.

Fragmentation The breaking down or decentralization among many individuals and policymakers in today's interest group universe.

Grass-roots lobbying A process whereby organizations take a series of actions to catalyze their members with respect to certain policies under consideration.

Group entrepreneur A charismatic individual possessing strong organizational skills and capable of energizing certain citizen-action organizations.

Informal rule making A process of devising administrative rules that can have broad application for many citizens.

Interest group An aggregation of citizens with shared interests and with common political aspirations or objectives, especially where public policymaking is concerned.

Iron triangle Enduring relationships between interest group, administrative, and congressional personnel as far as certain public policies are concerned.

Issue network Ongoing and informal interactions between public officials and private individuals over specific policies.

Latent interest Certain interests that can be activated as a result of actions or policy positions taken by government.

Lobbyist A paid representative who communicates constituent policy concerns to various public officials.

Monetary policy National policies designed to maintain economic growth and stability through credit, money supplies, and interest rates.

Negative advertising (campaigning) Campaign ads or literature questioning the behavior or opinions and actions of one's political opponent.

Party-in-government Incumbent Republicans and Democrats.

Political action committees (PACs) A combination of citizens that voluntarily donates to political campaigns, usually at the behest of a sponsor (corporation or labor union).

Political party An association of like-minded citizens joining together to nominate and elect supporters to government and thereby influence public policy.

Potential groups Individuals recognizing some general common interest among themselves but not formally organized.

Progressives A turn-of-the-century middle-class reform movement that sought to eliminate existing political corruption and malfeasance through an established merit system, the secret ballot, and greater public accountability by officeholders.

Redistributive policy A policy that transfers wealth and other existing resources from one group or class to another.

Regulatory policy Public policies establishing guidelines or limits with respect to both individuals and organizations in society.

***Reproductive Health Services* v. *Webster* (1989)** A major case dealing with the right of a state to place certain special limitations on women seeking an abortion.

***Roe* v. *Wade* (1973)** A major Supreme Court case establishing the right of a woman to terminate a pregnancy under the concept of "the right to privacy."

Selective benefits Goods or services limited to members of a certain organization or interest group.

Soft money Political contributions or disbursements by the major parties to state parties for various party-building activities such as voter registration, get-out-the-vote drives, and other related activities.

Spoils system A comprehensive system by the majority party of distributing jobs and other benefits to supporters of the victorious party. "To the victors go the spoils of office."

Statutory intent Goals and/or objectives of Congress outlined in legislation and intended as instructions to various policymaking agencies or arenas.

Strategies Various preconceived plans of action aimed at achieving victory in the ongoing political game.

Targeting Communicating specifically drafted messages to a specific segment of the population.

References

WORLD WIDE WEB

An increasing number of sites on the World Wide Web are now available for searching and researching materials on both American government and political interest groups. Below one will find a number of sites on the Web that can serve as "gateways" for subjects both governmental and political. Of course, one must keep in mind that sources available are determined by one's software and services used such as Compuserve, Prodigy, or America On Line.

Some gateways that deal with American government generally include:

Internet Public Library   http://ipl.sils.umich.edu/

Jefferson Project   http://www.stardot.com/jefferson/

Politics Now   http://www.politicsnow.com/

Yahoo/Government   http://www.yahoo.com/Government/

Specific Internet sources on each branch of the federal government include:

Congress

Senate   http://www.senate.gov

Hearing schedule   http://www.senate.gov/activities/hearing.html

House of Representatives   http://www.house.gov

Hearing schedule   http://thomas.loc.gov/home/hcomso.html

White House and Bureaucracy

White House   http://www.whitehouse.gov./WH/Welcome.html

(Library of Congress as a source)

http://lcweb.loc.gov/global/executive/fed.html

(Federal Web Locator for bureaucracy)

http://www.law.vill.edu./Fedwebloc.html

http://www.doc.gov/

Supreme Court

http://supct.law.cornell.du/suspct

(oral arguments before the Supreme Court)

http://oyez.at.nwu.edu/oyez.html

Internet Sources for Political Interest Groups

Capital Source
http://politicsusa.com/PoliticsUSA/CapSource/Source_1.html,cgi

Labor Net   http://www.igc.apc.org/labornet/

Yahoo/Public Interest Groups   http://www.yahoo.com/
Economy/Organizations/Public_Interest_Group

It should also be noted that some political interest groups have their own Web page. Some examples are the following:

American Federation of Labor
http://www.aflcio.org

Christian Coalition
http://www.cc.org

Common Cause
http://www.commoncause.org

Mothers Against Drunk Driving
http://www.madd.org

National Association for the Advancement of Colored People
http://www.naacp.org

National Organization for Women
http://www.now.org

National Rifle Association
http://www.nra.org

BOOKS

Baer, Denise L., and David A. Bositis, *Politics and Linkage in a Democratic Society.* Upper Saddle River, NJ: Prentice Hall, 1993.

Bentley, Arthur F., *Process of Government.* Chicago: University of Chicago Press, 1908.

Bernstein, Marver, *Regulating Business by Independent Commission*, Princeton, NJ: Princeton University Press, 1955.

Berry, Jeffery M., *The Interest Group Society,* 3rd ed. New York: Longman, 1997.

Birnbaum, Jefferey, and Alan S. Murray, *Showdown at Gucci Gulch: Lawmakers, Lobbyists and the Unlikely Triumph of Tax Reform.* New York: Random House, 1987.

Bolling, Richard, *House Out of Order.* New York: Harper and Row, 1965.

Browne, William P., *Private Interests, Public Policy, and American Agriculture.* Lawrence: University of Kansas Press, 1988.

Burnham, Walter Dean, *Democracy in the Making.* Upper Saddle River, NJ: Prentice Hall, 1983.

Cigler, Allan J., and Burdett A. Loomis, *Interest Group Politics,* 3rd ed. Washington, DC: CQ Press, 1991.

Clawson, Dan, Alan Newstandtl and Denise Scott, *Money Talks: Corporate PACs and Policy.* New York: Basic Books, 1992.

Connally, W. E., *Terms of Political Discourse.* Lexington, MA: D. C. Heath, 1974.

Craig, Barbara Hinkson, and David M. O'Brien, *Abortion and American Politics.* Chatham, NJ: Chatham House, 1993.

Cronin, Thomas E., *The State of the Presidency.* Boston: Little, Brown, 1980.

Culhane, Paul J., *Public Lands Politics: Interest Group Influence on the Forest Service and Bureau of Land Management.* Baltimore, MD: Johns Hopkins University Press, 1981.

Dahl. Robert, *Who Governs?* New Haven, CT: Yale University Press, 1961.

Davidson, Roger H., and Walter J. Oleszek, *Congress and Its Members,* 5th ed. Washington, DC: CQ Press, 1996.

Deakin, James, *The Lobbyists.* Washington, DC: Public Affairs Press, 1966.

Drew, Elizabeth, *Politics and Money: The New Road to Corruption.* New York: Macmillan, 1983.

Eismeier, Theodore, and Phillip H. Pollack, *Money, Business and the Rise of Corporate PACs in American Politics.* New York: Quorum Books, 1988.

Epstein, Lee, *Conservatives in Court.* Knoxville: University of Tennessee Press, 1985.

Epstein, Lee, and Joseph F. Kobylks, *The Supreme Court and Legal Change.* Chapel Hill: University of North Carolina Press, 1992.

Fenno, Richard F., *Congressmen in Committees.* Boston: Little, Brown, 1973.

Gais, Thomas, *Improper Influence: Campaign Finance Law, Political Interest Groups, and the Problem of Equality.* Ann Arbor: University of Michigan Press, 1996.

Gray, Osha Davidson, *Under Fire: The NRA and the Battle for Gun Control.* New York: Holt, 1993.

Heinz, John P., Edward O. Laumann, Robert L. Nelson, and Robert H. Salisbury, *The Hollow Core: Private Interests in National Policy Making.* Cambridge, MA: Harvard University Press, 1993.

Hoftstader, Richard, *The Age of Reform.* New York: Random House, 1955.

Jacobson, Gary, *Money in Congressional Elections.* New Haven, CT: Yale University Press, 1980.

Key, V. O., *The Responsible Electorate.* New York: Random House, 1966.

Landy, Mark K., Marc J. Roberts, and Stephen R. Thomas, *The Environmental Protection Agency: Asking the Wrong Questions from Nixon to Clinton.* New York: Oxford University Press, 1994.

Lindbloom, Charles, *Politics and Markets.* New York: Basic Books, 1977.

Lowi, Theodore, *The End of Liberalism.* New York: W. W. Norton, 1979.

Lukes, Steven, *Power: A Radical View.* London: Macmillan, 1974.

Lunch, William M., *The Nationalization of American Politics.* Berkeley: University of California Press, 1987.

Mahood, Harry R., *Interest Group Politics in America: A New Intensity.* Upper Saddle River, NJ.: Prentice Hall, 1990.

Mann, Thomas E., and Norman J. Ornstein, eds., *The New Congress.* Washington, DC: American Enterprise Institute, 1981.

Mansbridge, Jane J., *Why We Lost the ERA*. Chicago: University of Chicago Press, 1986.

Matthews, Donald R., *U.S. Senators and Their World*. Chapel Hill: University of North Carolina Press, 1960.

McConnell, Grant, *Private Power and American Democracy*. New York: Vintage Books, 1967.

McFarland, Andrew, *Common Cause*. Chatham, NJ: Chatham House, 1984.

McIntyre, Robert S., J. M. Crystal, and David C. Wilhelm, *The Corporate Tax Comeback: Corporate Income Taxes After Tax Reform*. Washington, DC: Citizens For Tax Justice, 1986.

McIntyre, Robert S., and Jeff Spinner, *130 Reasons Why We Need Tax Reform*. Washington, DC: Citizens for Tax Justice, 1996.

Michels, Roberto, *Political Parties: A Sociological Study of Oligarchical Trends of Modern Democracy*. New York: Crowell-Collier, 1916/1962.

Morehouse, Sara McCally, *State Politics, Parties and Policy*. New York: Holt, Rinehart and Winston, 1981.

Olson, Mancur, *The Logic of Collective Action*. Boston: Harvard University Press, 1965.

Ornstein, Norman, and Shirley Elder, *Interest Groups, Lobbying and Policymaking*, Washington, DC: CQ Press, 1978.

Ornstein, Norman, Thomas E. Mann, and Michael J. Malbin, eds., *Vital Statistics on Congress*. Washington, DC: CQ Press, 1994.

Orwell, George, *Animal Farm*. New York: Harcourt Brace, 1946.

Pateman, Carole, *Political Participation and Democracy*. Cambridge, U.K.: Cambridge University Press, 1970.

Pertschuck, Michael, *Revolt Against Regulation: The Rise and Pause of the Consumer Movement*. Berkeley: University of California Press, 1982.

Ranney, Austin, *Governing: An Introduction to Political Science*. Upper Saddle River, NJ: Prentice Hall, 1990.

Rosenbaum, Walter A., *Environmental Politics and Policy*. Washington, DC: CQ Press, 1995.

Ryden, David K., *Representation in Crisis: The Constitution, Interest Groups, and Political Parties*. Albany: State University Press of New York, 1996.

Schattschneider, E. E., *Party Government*. New York: Farrar and Rinehart, 1942.

Schattschneider, E. E., *Semi-Sovereign People*. New York: Holt, Rinehart and Winston, 1961.

Schlozman, Kay, and John Tierney, *Organized Interests and American Democracy*. New York: Harper and Row, 1986.

Spitzer, Robert J., *The Politics of Gun Control*. Chatham, NJ: Chatham House, 1995.

Stern, Philip M., *Still the Best Congress Money Can Buy.* Washington, DC: Regenry Gateway, 1992.

Taylor, Peter, *The Smoking Ring.* New York: Mentor Books, 1985.

Tocqueville, Alexis de, *Democracy in America.* New York: Colonial Press, 1899.

Truman, David, *The Governmental Process.* New York: Knopf, 1951.

Walker, Jack, *Mobilizing Interest Groups in America: Parties, Professionals, and Social Movement.* Ann Arbor: University of Michigan Press, 1991.

Welch, Susan, John Gruhl, Michael Steinman, John Comer, and Susan Rigdon, *American Government,* 5th ed. Minneapolis, MN: West Publishing Company, 1994.

Wolinsky, Harold, and Tom Brune, *The Serpent on the Staff: The Unhealthy Politics of the American Medical Association.* New York: Jeremy P. Tarcher/Putnam Books, 1994.

Wolpe, Bruce C., and Bertram J. Levine, *Lobbying Congress: How the System Works,* 2nd ed. Washington, DC: CQ Press, 1996.

Wright, John R., *Interest Groups in Congress: Lobbying, Contributions and Influence.* Boston: Allyn and Bacon, 1996.

Zorack, John, L., *The Lobbying Handbook: A Comprehensive Lobbying Guide.* Washington, DC: Professional Lobbying and Consulting Center, 1990.

ARTICLES AND PERIODICALS

AFL-CIO News, April 29, 1987.

Bachrach, S., and Morton Baratz, "Two Faces of Power," *APSR* 56 (1962), pp. 947–952.

Behuniak-Long, Susan. "Friendly Fire: Amici Curia and *Webster v Reproductive Health Services*," *Judicature* 74 (1991), pp. 260–269.

Birnbaum, Jeffrey, "Kings of K Street," *Fortune Magazine,* December 7, 1998, p. 137.

Birnbaum, Jeffrey, "The Fallen Giant," *Fortune Magazine,* December 8, 1997, pp. 156-157.

Calderia, Gregory A., and John R. Wright, "Amici Curiae Before the Supreme Court: Who Participates, When and How Much?" *JOP* 52 (1990), pp. 782–806.

Cardozo Law Review 9 (1987), pp. 187–200.

Daly, John, and Jennifer Keen, "Beyond the Limits: Soft Money in the 1996 Elections," *Center for Responsive Politics* (1997).

DeGregorio, Christine, and Jack Rossotti, "Resources, Attitudes and Strategies: Interest Group Participation in the Bork Confirmation Process." *American Review of Politics,* 15, (1994), pp. 1-19.

Dewhirst, R. E. "Unusual Allies: Bipartisanship and the Passage of NAFTA." Unpublished paper, National Social Science Association Meeting, April 5–7, 1996, San Diego.

Frankfurter, Felix, "The Supreme Court and the Public," *Forum* 83 (1930), pp. 330–339.

Krislov, Samuel. "The Supreme Court and the Public, From Friendship to Advocacy," *Yale Law Review* 72 (1963), pp. 703–705b.

Livingston, Barbara, "Physician-Assisted Suicide—Is It a Constitutional Right?" *Bioethics Bulletin* (Spring/Summer 1997), pp. 2–11.

Martino, Ann M., and Cynthia Cates Colella, contributors,"The Transformation in American Politics: Implications for Federalism," (Commission Report) (Washington, DC: Advisory Commission on Intergovernmental Relations, 1986) Chapter 6.

O'Brien, David M. "The Reagan Judges: His Most Enduring Legacy?" in *The Reagan Legacy: Promise and Performance,* Charles O. Jones, ed. Chatham, NJ: Chatham House, 1988, pp. 60–99.

Orman, John. "The President and Interest Group Access." *Presidential Studies Quarterly* XVIII (1988), pp. 787–791.

Ratnesar, Romesh, and John Cook, "Oil Slick," *Mother Jones* (May/June 1997).

Schlozman, Kay, "Voluntary Organizations in Politics: Who Gets Involved?" in *Representing Interests and Interest Group Representation,* William Crotty, Mildred A. Schwartz, and John C. Green, eds. Lanham, MD: University Press of America, 1991.

Schlozman, Kay, and J. T. Tierney, "More of the Same: Washington Pressure Group Activity in a Decade of Change," *JOP* 45 (1983), pp. 351–375.

Sorauf, Frank, "Political Action Committees in American Politics: An Overview," in *What Price PACS?* Washington, DC: Twentieth Century Fund, 1984, pp. 30–42.

Sorauf, Frank, "Who's in Charge? Accountability in Political Action Committees." *PSQ* 99 (1984), pp. 591-614.

Stone, Peter, "From the K Street Corridor," *National Journal,* October 26,1996, p. 2297.

Tierney, John, testimony before the Senate Committee on Governmental Affairs, and quoted in "The Transformation in American Politics," Washington, DC: Advisory Commission on Intergovernmental Relations, 1986, Chapter 6.

Index